THE
MENTALIST'S
HANDBOOK

THE
MENTALIST'S
HANDBOOK

An Explorer's Guide to
Astral, Spirit, and Psychic Worlds

CLINT MARSH

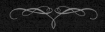

Foreword and Illustrations by Jeff Hoke,
author of *The Museum of Lost Wonder*

WEISERBOOKS
San Francisco, CA / Newburyport, MA

First published in 2008 by
Red Wheel/Weiser, LLC
With offices at:
500 Third Street, Suite 230
San Francisco, CA 94107
www.redwheelweiser.com

Library of Congress Cataloging-in-Publication Data

Marsh, Clint, 1974-
  The mentalist's handbook : an explorer's guide to astral, spirit, and
psychic worlds / Clint Marsh ; illustrations by Jeff Hoke.
      p. cm.
  Includes index.
  ISBN 978-1-57863-421-7 (alk. paper)
  1. Parapsychology. 2. Occultism. I. Hoke, Jeff. II. Title.
  BF1031.M3485 2008
  133.8—dc22
                                        2007048230

Cover and text design by Donna Linden
Typeset in Caslon and LDecoration Pi
Cover and text illustrations © Jeff Hoke

Printed in China
MD
10 9 8 7 6 5 4 3

"*The Human Soul possesses, from the fact of its being of the same essence as all creation, a marvellous power. One who possesses the secret is enabled to rise as high as his imagination will carry him; but he does that only on the condition of becoming closely united to this universal force.*"

—HEINRICH CORNELIUS AGRIPPA,
de Occulta Philosophia
(trans. H. P. Blavatsky, *Isis Unveiled*)

CONTENTS

*The Basics of Meditation and Visualization—The Basics of
Meditation—An Initial Meditation— The Basics of Visualization—
A Simple Visualization—The Importance of Imagination—
A Description of the Aetheric Plane—Imagining the Aetheric Plane—
The Location of This Place—"What Good Is the Aetheric Plane?"—
The Nature of Aether—Aether as a Substance—The Sculptor's
Studio—Some Questions about the Sculptor's Studio—Aether and the
Supernatural World—Two Bodies in One Person—Visualizing the
Aetheric Body—Visualization and Memory—Observation and
Memory—Memory of the Commonplace—The Mentalism
Connection—Psychisms—Astral Projection—Spiritism—Mind Is
Matter, Matter Is Mind—Letters from Aspirants*

*The Aetheric Plane, Its Worlds and Vibrations—The Astral World—
The Elemental World—The Elysian World, or Elysium—An
Introduction to Vibrational Theory—All Is Aether—Below and above
the Material—Elemental Vibration—Perception and Reality in the
Aether—Inky Flares—An Aetheric Bestiary—Animal Spirits—Astral
Hounds—Departed Spirits—Devas—The Dweller on the Threshold—*

ILLUSTRATIONS

FOREWORD

CLINT AND I SHARE A SECRET. It's a secret that's difficult to describe, even to ourselves. It comes from a hidden desire to believe in the unknown, mixed with a particular skepticism. We believe there's more out there than what reasonable people have answers for, but the realities of everyday life reinforce our pragmatism. We experience things in life that mystify us, we read, we talk it over, and we try to make sense of it all through what we create. Belief spurs creativity. Creativity beckons belief. It'd be a pretty dreary world without either.

I first met Clint at the Alternative Press Expo in San Jose, California, in 1999. I was there exhibiting the first physical manifestation of the Museum of Lost Wonder, a velvet-curtained facade hovering over a few of my early pamphlets. The show surrounded me with a dizzying array of young artists spewing forth their cartoon characters. I didn't quite fit in.

Somehow my own brand of quirkiness attracted Clint. He introduced himself and shared a few jokes. He didn't seem to fit in either. Clint exuded warmth and a peculiar sense of humor (one immediately recognizable to fellow Midwesterners). Two weeks later he showed up on my doorstep, a hundred miles away, to talk to me about my work. We became fast friends.

Clint was, and still is, an amazing mixture of magic and common sense. He and I share a sense of wonder inherited from metaphysical books, Fortean magazines, and adventure comics that infected our minds as kids. It's a bug we never shook as we passed into adulthood. The enchantment has never gone away. Walking the thin line between reason and belief is what has drawn us together. The mystery, the work, has always been in reconciling the seemingly contradictory worlds of imagination and day-to-day life. To accomplish this we had to make worlds of our own where it all worked together. I created a world contained within a museum that, although it is a fantasy, is a very real place for me. Clint was able to materialize his world in the aether. Where I created a specific place in the imagination, Clint explores an entire region—one that is very real to many people—and gives us a kind of road map of how to get there. I think my museum lies somewhere on that plane.

Clint's work is a personal exploration into the unknown, one where all he's read, experienced, and wondered about makes sense. We had a heart-to-heart talk once, trying to figure out if this personal kind of investigation has any value for others. It was one of those "Why do we do this?", "Who cares?", and "Why does it matter?" conversations. We talked about finding our inspiration in the writings and ideas of esoteric thinkers throughout history. Thinking about those who came before—with their meandering, obfuscated, sometimes enlightening, oftentimes frustrating texts—made us realize our link to the past.

From the Neo-Platonists and Renaissance thinkers to the turn-of-the-century visionaries who combined Eastern and Western thought, intrepid pioneers of the imagination have always mixed personal fact and fancy in their philosophies (despite what they might want us to believe). They tried to make sense of the writings that inspired them. They mixed what these books taught them with their own personal experience, and they made their passions meaningful by sharing and expressing their ideas in terms of their own time. They syncretized and manifested esoteric thought into something meaningful, something useful. They did, in their own eras, the same thing we are doing now.

Clint has emulated a style that nods to the past, but his pragmatic approach is totally modern. If our work has any value, it's in our being part of this continuum of idealists who have reached into the past, embraced the present, and tried to carry their inspiration into the world they lived in.

Clint was the first editor of my writings for *The Museum of Lost Wonder,* and he continues to help make sense of my creations. I'm proud to have drawn the pictures that help give life to the very practical, but uncommon, sense you'll find in the book you're reading now.

The secret Clint and I share remains difficult to describe, but at its heart it's that we believe everyone has the ability to suspend disbelief, explore the imagination, and apply what they find to everyday life. The secret is out there for everyone to discover and make their own. Here is a guidebook. Enjoy the adventure.

Jeff Hoke

INTRODUCTION

WHEN I BEGAN WORK ON THE ESSAYS that would eventually be collected in *The Mentalist's Handbook,* my intention was to create a starting point for discussion and investigation into the world's more inexplicable phenomena, those things we ponder but can't explain through thinking alone. I'd been fascinated with the power of the human mind and its purported ability for astral projection, communication with the spirit world, and psychic feats for as long as I could remember, reading any related books I got my hands on and talking to whomever would share with me stories of their own experiences. I was sure there was a reason for such phenomena to exist, and I had a sense that it was all related somehow. But no one could explain any of it to my satisfaction. Could this all be true? I was insecure, too, about being called a fool for questioning the limits of human knowledge in the rational world that we live in today.

Eventually my frustration got the upper hand, and I took it upon myself to build a home for all things unexplainable. Using a combination of visualization techniques, art class exercises, ideas from esoteric books, and healthy doses of intuition and imagination, I forged a place called the aetheric plane, a realm that could be explored through the contemplative practice known as mentalism. Strange as it may seem, I wasn't the first person to visit the aether. The Theosophists of the Victorian era and other thinkers throughout history had been there before me, so when I began publishing a series of pamphlets about my own take on the aether, my writing and production styles were in homage to those who had gone before. Each issue of *The Camelopard* explored a different aspect of this fantastic realm. My love of the authoritative voice of secret society publications, combined with my own anxieties about my interest in these strange topics, led me to write in the grandiose style of a master mentalist, one who already had all the answers. To my surprise and delight, letters from around the world began to come to me in response to the pamphlets. It seemed I was far from alone in my search for answers.

Throughout this project's decadelong development, I've gone back and forth constantly in my mind about what I really think about mentalism and the aetheric plane. Just like the aether itself, my own approach to this material is an ungraspable blend of the concrete and the imaginary. My exploration style has been that of the enthusiastic amateur, a self-made scholar taking perilous leaps between other people's investigations and my own experience and instincts. My thesis has been built up through accretion, osmosis, and the weird alchemy that goes on in each of our imaginations. I've maintained my skepticism every step of the way, yet whenever I try any of the experiments in this book, I gain real and valuable insight into the power and workings of the human mind and, in doing so, of the aether itself. I suppose the Wizard of Oz has days like this, too.

If attempted with dedication and openness, this coursework will leave no one unchanged. Some of you will perceive the world of the aether exactly the way it is described in this book, in all its fantastic strangeness. Others of you will gain a deeper understanding of your capacity for memory and visualization. The aether manifests itself in subtle ways and never exactly how we expect.

I am sincerely interested in reading accounts of your own experiences with the various aspects of the aetheric plane, either through the techniques presented in *The Mentalist's Handbook* or using other methods. Please feel free to send written correspondence to me at the postal address below or via my Web site, *www.wonderella.org*, which has current information about *The Camelopard* and other publications. Thank you very much for your interest in the aether. I wish you the best of luck in your explorations.

Clint Marsh
Post Office Box 10145
Berkeley, California 94709

THE CAMELOPARD

AT THE HEIGHT OF THEIR GLORY, the ancient Romans controlled vast amounts of Europe, Asia, and Africa. Merchants brought wonders from the far reaches of the empire to Rome to be displayed for the enjoyment of the emperor and the public alike.

One of these wonders they called the camelopard—a creature with the head of a camel and the spots of a leopard. Now known as the giraffe, this graceful, elevated animal evoked a sense of mystery and wonder in its day. This fine beast serves as the mascot for aspiring mentalists.

By bringing far-flung knowledge before the public, this book's author hopes to inform and enlighten in the manner of the merchants of ancient Rome. *The Mentalist's Handbook* endeavors to explain to the common man the nature and practice of mentalism and of the aetheric plane, which makes possible extraordinary feats including astral projection, spirit communication, and psychic powers.

As you study this book you will gain insight into the aetheric plane through general theory, historical examples, everyday comparisons, and easy-to-follow exercises. It is hoped that, as an aspiring mentalist, you will attempt the exercises to the best of your ability and contact the author to tell of the results.

INSTRUCTIONS FOR
RECORDING EXPERIMENTS

AS YOU LEARN ABOUT AETHER, it is important to keep a record of the exact methods and results of your experiments in mentalism. Outlined here are instructions for recording such experiments. Aspiring mentalists should follow the instructions as closely as possible and send a copy of the results to the author.

Just as a carpenter cannot build a house without a hammer and nails, so the mentalist cannot faithfully record his or her experiments without the proper tools. Perhaps the most important tool in the recording of aetheric experiments—beyond pen and paper—is the secretary. The secretary need not be in your employ, per se. He or she may be a friend of yours, ideally one who shares your interest in mentalism. The secretary's role is to sit nearby and faithfully record the exact goings-on during your experiments.

If no secretary is forthcoming, and your funds allow, you might consider placing an advertisement for one in the classifieds section of your local newspaper. Or you could buy a tape recorder.

It is crucial that your early experiments be recorded as faithfully as possible. Communicate the need for clarity and thoroughness to your secretary before the two of you commence recording.

Each record should include a brief synopsis of your general state of mind (calm, agitated, etc.), your diet for the past twenty-four hours, any thoughts weighing heavily on your mind, and any abnormal external conditions that may affect your session, such as a thunderstorm, a change in venue for your meditations, or anything else like this.

When this is done and you are ready, signal to your secretary (or turn on your tape recorder) and begin your aetheric session the way you would any other. If you are using pen and paper to record, try not to break from your experiment to jot down your thoughts; rather, wait until the experiment is over. If you are recording via tape or secretary, you may make commentary aloud for a better account of the session. The secretary should take note of any shift in temperature, weather, or other atmospheric conditions as they occur. Relax and go through your session as you would normally, but bearing in mind that you must clearly remember what happens so as to better compare your impressions to the recorded account.

When you are through, mentally review your recorded account for accuracy. Add as much detail as you can and whatever conclusions you draw from the experiment.

The author is glad to receive copies of your recorded experiments, as well as general questions or commentary on the material in this course of study. Correspondents should include their full name and address. Mail all manuscripts via post or electronic mail using the contact information given in this book's introduction.

IMAGINATION—VISUALIZATION—REALIZATION

REMEMBER! ALL IS AETHER

MENTALISM = WILL OVER AETHER

THE
MENTALIST'S
HANDBOOK

'A voice crying in the wilderness'

VOX CLAMANTIS IN DESERTO

LESSON ONE.
THE NATURE OF AETHER

The Basics of Meditation and Visualization—The Basics of Meditation—An Initial Meditation—The Basics of Visualization— A Simple Visualization—The Importance of Imagination—A Description of the Aetheric Plane—Imagining the Aetheric Plane— The Location of This Place—"What Good Is the Aetheric Plane?"— The Nature of Aether—Aether as a Substance—The Sculptor's Studio—Some Questions about the Sculptor's Studio—Aether and the Supernatural World—Two Bodies in One Person—Visualizing the Aetheric Body—Visualization and Memory—Observation and Memory—Memory of the Commonplace—The Mentalism Connection—Psychisms—Astral Projection—Spiritism—Mind Is Matter, Matter Is Mind—Letters from Aspirants

"Little brother, give me thy hand; for the first step is hard."
—ALEISTER CROWLEY

ABOVE, BELOW, AND THROUGHOUT the world you and I call home, the aetheric plane dwells also. Everything we see, hear, touch, think, and feel has a counterpart in this place, and when you visit the aetheric plane, you will see how the material and mental qualities of these things begin to blur and intermingle. "Aether" is the word used to signify the substance that makes up the aetheric plane.

In this lesson, the qualities of aether and the aetheric plane are set, to form a foundation for exploration into this vast and fascinating realm. You will learn much more than you thought you would and think more than you knew you could. Your curiosity will be set alight, and you will dare to pierce the veil between this world and the others.

Using the simple exercises described in this lesson, your faculty for mentalism will increase. Don't be discouraged if at first you are not as successful as you like with the lessons. All will be yours through practice and diligence.

And now, let us proceed with our worthy goal, informing the world of the facts surrounding the nature of aether.

THE BASICS OF MEDITATION AND VISUALIZATION

Meditation and visualization are two important practices used in the exercises in the rest of this book. They are the first skills anyone aspiring to mentalism must learn. These pages will introduce you to the concepts behind meditation and visualization and will lead you through preliminary trials of both.

The Basics of Meditation

Meditation is the root skill of the aspiring mentalist. By relaxing us and shifting our attention from the everyday, meditation is the tool that allows us to connect to the aetheric plane. In order for meditation to be effective, it must be practiced daily. These directions will help you with your first simple meditations. As your aetheric studies progress, you will learn much more about this skill.

If this were a book for bodybuilders, it would include exercises for you to repeat to strengthen your physical muscles. We are going to strengthen our "mental muscles" the same way weight-lifters build their biceps—through practice! You will find that frequent meditation on a certain thing (in this exercise we'll focus on the breath) will help you concentrate your thoughts and relax your body. A calm mind and body are essential to mentalism.

Exercise 1: An Initial Meditation

Find a quiet space where you can go and not be disturbed by noise or others. Sit in a chair or on the floor, in a comfortable position but with your back straight. Meditation is about breathing, and with a straight back, you allow your lungs optimal expansion. If you are in a chair, you can resist the temptation to slouch by sitting on its front edge.

Relax. Concentrate on your breath. Breathe slowly and deliberately, letting yourself relax more and more. Try to think only of your breath as it enters, fills, and exits your body. It may help to close your eyes.

Although it is not necessary to time your meditation, you should concentrate on your breathing for about five minutes. This will grant you a deeper attention to your body and the physical act of breathing.

If you find your attention wavering from your breath, gently return your thoughts to the simple rhythm of the air flowing in and out of your body. Don't be frustrated if you get distracted again and again, especially if you are new to meditation. This takes practice. With time, meditation will come more and more naturally to you. Continue to breathe slowly—with your mind focused on your breath—for another five minutes, ten if you're enjoying it.

When you are through, stand up from your sitting position and stretch, letting your attention come back to the world around you. Repeat this type of meditation for fifteen minutes at least once every day. If you do, you will develop your ability to concentrate on something very intently (in this case your breath) while entering a relaxed state of being. Just as important, you will find yourself happier and more relaxed in general. All these traits are essential to mentalism.

The Basics of Visualization

Perhaps the most versatile skill of the mentalist is visualization, the ability to see with the mind's eye things not readily visible to the physical eye. Visualizations are used by mentalists to help them picture the aetheric plane. This is how you will use visualization at first, seeing the aetheric plane in your imagination. Later, it will be the tool you use to see aether for what it truly is.

Taken at face value, visualization is written off by many as pure imagination. At first this is true. Visualization, for beginners, is little more than concentration on certain thoughts to the point that those thoughts are integrated into the real scene before the mentalist. In mentalism and aetheric studies in general, visualization is an important skill to practice, because it is the first step on the road to true sensing and interaction with aether.

Exercise 2: A Simple Visualization

Here is an elementary visualization that you can perform even if you are new to the discipline. This exercise works in part because of certain physical principles that govern the eye. It is based on an *optical illusion.*

Sit in a room with a white or light-colored wall. Stare at the simple geometric figure of the hand while counting slowly to thirty, then quickly shift your gaze to the aforementioned wall. It may help if you blink rapidly when you do.

Do you see the afterimage of the figure upon the wall, the white parts black and the black parts white? The effect is caused by a physical afterimage left upon your eyes from staring so long at the image and is an example of your mind interpreting the

afterimage as a picture that is really before your eyes. This is a shadowy start to your visualizations but a start nonetheless.

Do this a few more times, then take this little leap: Try to *visualize* the same image upon the wall. Can you see it without staring at the illustration first? Try it now. It's all right if you can't at first, but you should keep practicing this to develop your visualization abilities.

The difference between the first and second way of seeing the image is that the second time you are seeing without the aid of any physical stimulus. You are using your mind. Compare the two styles of seeing by practicing both, then see if you can play with your visualizations. Can you visualize the shape against different walls? Can you visualize it suspended out from the wall a bit? Can you add parts to the image, maybe extra fingers, for example, and then take them away? If so, good for you! You are well on your way to more complex visualizations.

The Importance of Imagination

As you practice the visualization exercises in this lesson, you will realize just how crucial imagination is to the work. Don't think of imagination as a crutch, something you have to overcome to get to "real" visualizations. Imagination is less like a roadblock to visualization and more like a map. You've been imagining things all your life, and visualization is an ability very akin to imagination.

A DESCRIPTION OF THE AETHERIC PLANE

To the question I am often asked—"What is the aetheric plane like?"—I respond with a question of my own: "How can one describe such a place?" The answer to the second question is, "Not nearly enough."

The simplest way to put it is this: There is another world beyond, yet inside, the material world you and I know and inhabit. This place is at once different from and the same as ours. Everything in this other world looks as though it is made of light. In fact, all things on the aetheric plane are made of a superfine substance known as aether.

Given the newness of your interest and studies, were you to see the aetheric plane now, put plainly, you would go mad. It is best to start with a visualization of this place. As you progress through the exercises in this and further lessons, you will find that visualizations are second only to realizations, so heed this exercise carefully.

Exercise 3: Imagining the Aetheric Plane
Here is an exercise to help you envision the aetheric plane in relation to the material world we inhabit. It involves creating an aetheric scene that corresponds with the landscape you are already in. The first few times you perform this exercise, simply use your imagination to picture the scenes. Once you feel comfortable with your visualization skills, you should try this exer-

cise again for a heightened sense of the omnipresence of the aetheric plane.

When you are an accomplished mentalist, you will be able to see and interact with aetheric landscapes. The tools you will use will be those of the mentalist—visualization, clairvoyance, and astral projection. For now, however, you will be instructed in this exercise using a tool you already possess: imagination. It might be helpful for a friend to read the following text to you while you do this, as most of it is done with your eyes closed.

Take a look out your window or, if you are fortunate enough to be reading this outdoors, across the furthest landscape available to you. This place that you see before you exists in tandem on the aetheric plane. Examine it in detail. Note the dimensions of the scene before you—the height, breadth, and depth of the landscape. What are the main features of the scene? What are the little details that take some time to notice?

When you are satisfied that you have a good idea of the lay of the land, take a deep breath. Let it out slowly and close your eyes. Picture the scene that you just took in through your sense of vision. Think about the dimensions of height, breadth, and depth. Remember the features you noted and fit them into the landscape in your mind.

This mental landscape is not the same as the scene before you—it is a product of your imagination. Continue to breathe deeply. Keep your eyes closed and scrutinize your mental visualization, adding as many objects as you can remember from the "real" landscape into your imaginary one.

When you think your mental landscape is as complete as you can make it, you will need to make one final change to it. The scene you have built in your mind is a section of the aetheric plane, a world that mirrors our own. In this place, everything seems to be made of light. Color everything in your mental landscape a light blue, or a yellow, or whatever color you fancy, so that it looks as if the whole scene has a translucent glow to it.

Now, holding your glowing mental landscape at the forefront of your thoughts, open your eyes and superimpose it over the actual scene, as if it were a translucent shell that wraps around all you see. If you can do this, you have already begun to develop your capacity for visualization.

The "double vision" you have created is imaginary, but there is more to what you are seeing than pure imagination. In reality, beyond the gross material of our world exists another world of wonder and possibility—the aetheric plane. It is a place and a feeling, a thought and an emotion, and all of these things at once. It is the sum total of reality and of life itself. It is the purest—and at the same time the most practical and real—incarnation of the stuff we call imagination.

The Location of This Place

Another question I often field in regards to the aetheric plane concerns its precise location. "Where could this fantastic realm be?" aspirants wonder aloud. The answer at first seems overly enigmatic: "The aetheric plane exists in many places at once."

It is important to realize that the "floating" location where we placed the aetheric plane in our visualization is just one of an infinite number of places to visualize the plane. As you learn more about the aetheric plane, you will more easily understand the omnipresence of this place.

Technically speaking, the aetheric plane is above, below, beside, and beyond our world, existing in all places at once, boundless and invisible, or at least invisible to you for now. The aetheric plane is experienced through a shift in consciousness brought on by meditation and visualization, and it is right here, within us, now. With practice, you will catch a glimpse of the aetheric plane, and before you know it, you will see it clearly.

"What Good Is the Aetheric Plane?"

This is a valid question, especially today, when time is a valuable commodity and so much of it is required for the study of aether and mentalism.

Here is your answer: Think back to every extraordinary story you have ever heard, every anecdote or legend that involved unusual beings or abilities. Recall every example of haunting, supernatural strength, déjà vu, or extrasensory perception. Do you know what common element is shared by all those stories, what factor lies behind the fantastic feats or occurrences described? If you haven't guessed it yet, know this: It is the aetheric plane.

All things tangible and intangible in this world—beings, objects, forces, thoughts, and emotions—are manifest on the aetheric plane in very substantial ways. There, a thought can be as mighty as a hurricane wind, destroying cities and ruining ecosystems. One person's emotion can profoundly affect another person's movement. A sound can build a civilization. An image can start a fire. All things are part of a common system, shared language understood by those tapped in to the power of the aetheric plane.

That said, the aetheric plane is not a place that can be known easily. Years of practice and study are required of aspirants to mentalism. The payoffs of this study are extraordinary. For if aether and the aetheric plane are part of a language, then those who speak that language fluently are no less than masters of reality.

Now can you see the good in learning of such a place?

THE NATURE OF AETHER

Some well-meaning aspirants to mentalism ask me, "What is aether made of?" Better for them to ask, "What isn't made of aether?" Answering the second question is much easier than answering the first.

Aether is all around us and within us as well. It surrounds and imbues our bodies, our atmospheres, and everything in between. Beneath the surface of our thoughts, our feelings, and our movements, aether lies. It is as alive as anything in the world, for in fact it constitutes everything in this world and beyond.

To explain something to a material person, one must use material terms. With this in mind, it is best to think of aether as a fluid, one that inhabits all space. This fluid is infinitely malleable and can change its color and density, so that it may look and feel like anything imaginable. Furthermore, the way one person perceives aether is quite often very different from the way another person does. A slippery substance indeed.

But aether is more than just a substance. It is also a force, like wind or ocean currents, like magnetism or infatuation. It is a force that can be gentler than a loving thought or more powerful than an apocalyptic storm, depending on how it is used.

In its natural state—or perhaps I should say in *our* natural state—aether is invisible and intangible. I stress that it is our natural state, the state of body and mind most people are in every day of their lives, that prevents us from seeing, touching, and otherwise actively experiencing aether.

The *natural* state of mankind is so called because of its connection to the "natural" material world and material awareness. The practice of mentalism elevates the physical and mental states of man to a higher level, from a *natural* state to a *supernatural* state, as it were, of aetheric awareness. Mentalism creates a shift in consciousness that opens our mind to the aetheric plane.

If you are at all familiar with the tenets of science, I am sure several alarms are now ringing in your mind. This talk of aether surely sounds too fantastic and unbelievable to be real. Everything we are taught about science refutes the theory of the aetheric plane, yet it is not scientists who bring us knowledge of aether, but mentalists. These men and women are pioneers in the newest and yet most ancient science: mentalism.

Whereas scientists and their hangers-on cannot see aether, trained mentalists see the stuff easily. As a mentalist, the world is your workshop as well as your playground. As a trained manipulator of aether—and hence of reality itself—the mentalist is one of the custodians of the world. To the mentalist, aether is the only thing of importance, because it is the basic substance of all substances.

Through strict practice of meditation and visualization, mentalists are able to manipulate aether to their will, each according to his or her level of expertise. Beginning mentalists are capable only of small feats of aether manipulation; those that continue their training eventually master marvels undreamed of by modern man. As you advance in your studies of aether and mentalism, your expertise will grow as well.

Everyone on earth has the potential to become a mentalist, but few follow the path. In matters of consciousness, mankind is a sleeping, dreaming bunch. Mentalism offers an awakening, an opening of eyes. Unfortunately, this awakening is a process that takes time and great effort, given the materialistic worldview we are born into.

When you finally see aether clearly and accept its place in your view of the cosmos, you will see the interconnectedness of all things. This is the goal of mentalism.

Aether as a Substance

Aether is a material that can assume any shape, texture, color, or density. As a substance, it is much finer than the air we breathe, finer than any element on the periodic table, finer even than any thought ever to pass through our minds.

Travelers to the aetheric plane find that this other world is composed of "doubles" of the places and beings found in our world. The things on the aetheric plane are ghostly in nature. It is as if the finest sheet of spider silk settled on all things on this earth, took the shape of what it touched, and floated away, all forms intact.

This is not to say that aether is a static material. No, it is constantly changing according to the will of mentalists practicing their skills. To the mentalist, aether is like a clay that can be sculpted by sheer willpower. Through intense concentration on a segment of the aetheric plane, a mentalist controls the form and feeling of the aether. And because aether embodies all things—objects, feelings, thoughts, actions—the mentalist who can manipulate aether thus controls these things as well.

Exercise 4: The Sculptor's Studio

This visualization exercise illustrates the richness and depth of the aetheric plane. First, just read the following description so you can understand the potential of aether and aetheric manipulation.

Later, you may want to visualize the scene and manipulate the aether in other ways. When you are ready to try this exercise as a true visualization, begin with at least ten minutes of breath meditation to relax you and clear your mind of jumbled thoughts of the everyday world. As with the other exercises in this book, you can have a friend read you the following description of the sculptor's studio while you visualize it.

If aether can be described as a substance much like clay, the mentalist can be described as a sculptor. Think of a busy sculptor's studio, one with huge masses of wet, malleable clay placed on tables throughout. Try to picture the studio as fully as you can, with many details. Take a while to connect with this imaginary place you are visualizing.

With this image set in your mind's eye, begin to change objects in the studio, one by one, to clay. The table the sculptor works at, for instance, changes, in your visualization, from wood and metal to clay. The studio floor becomes slick and permeable, ready to be molded. The walls, the windows, and the ceiling—all clay.

Now imagine the clothes of the sculptor changing to clay. The sculptor can form them into whatever costume he desires.

His flesh and bones and skin, his entire body, also shifts, to clay. Just as aether makes the whole of the aetheric plane, so clay composes all in this sculptor's studio.

All these things that are now clay can be approached by the sculptor, and each can be molded according to his desires. He may mold one of his hands into the form of a bird, detach it, and cause it to fly away. His other hand may be molded into the shape of a knife, and, without kiln or sunlight or even heat, the sculptor can harden this shape to the density of a knife much like one you or I would use to chop vegetables. With this knife he can slice through other pieces of aether, which, if your imagination has continued in the vein we began at the onset of this exercise, comprises now not only the physical objects in the studio. but

also the air, the shafts of sunlight coming in through the windows and all the dust in those shafts, the flight path of the hand/bird, and the thoughts and emotions of all sentient beings within the studio.

Spend some time in the sculptor's studio and have him alter the clay around himself. He can change it with ease, as if there were nothing to it. Anything can happen in his studio. Let your imagination run wild with the possibilities.

When you're ready to leave the studio, bring your thoughts back to your breath and meditate for at least five minutes before opening your eyes. This will give you time to internalize the possibilities inherent in aetheric manipulation.

Some Questions about the Sculptor's Studio

How could the sculptor mold his second hand, when his first has already flown away?

The answer to that question gets at the crux of the idea of aether. The man in this visualization is not actually a sculptor working with clay, *but a mentalist exercising his will over aether.* Material things, like hands and knives and birds, are manipulated by other material things. But because the sculptor was working not with clay but with aether, he is able to shape his second hand using mentalism, which by definition is "will over aether."

Let me clarify the question: If material objects need material manipulation, and aetheric objects need aetheric manipulation, how could the sculptor mold his second (aetheric) hand if his first (aetheric) hand is missing? Surely he needs aetheric tools in order to shape aether.

The only "aetheric tool" the sculptor (mentalist) requires is the power of his own mind, which he has developed through the practice of visualization. Remember that in addition to all visible things in the studio turning to clay (aether), all invisible things were turned as well. This includes the air, the thoughts of the sculptor, his emotions, and so on. Any of these "intangible" things could be manipulated just as easily as the "physical" objects in the room. To a mentalist, it makes no difference.

So did the sculptor need to change his second hand to a knife, or could he have used his mental ability to chop up aether instead?

This is a good point. It wasn't necessary for the sculptor to actually have an aetheric knife to use for aetheric manipulation. Sometimes, however, mentalists find it easier to visualize tools that they can use. This is a throwback to everyday materialistic perception of reality, but as we all live in the material world, that world carries over and influences the way we visualize the aetheric world.

Aether and the Supernatural World

Aether (and its malleability) is at the root of every so-called supernatural phenomenon. Think about it. With your new understanding of aether, it is easy to explain the existence of shape-shifters such as vampires and werewolves. These creatures are merely mentalists, ones who have specialized their ability to allow them to change their shape as well as their persona.

Does this make you more curious yet? All will come to be known in time. For now, know this about aether:

1. To the vast majority of people, aether is invisible, intangible, and imaginary. To mentalists, it is the only real thing in existence.
2. Aether is the whole of the aetheric plane. On the aetheric plane, all things—be they thoughts, things, energy, people, or what have you—are made of essentially the same stuff.
3. Aether is a substance that can be manipulated mentally.
4. The stronger the mental abilities of the mentalist, the stronger that mentalist's influence on the aetheric plane.

You too will be able to manipulate this substance, this life force, as you learn more of the power of mentalism.

TWO BODIES IN ONE PERSON

When you visit the aetheric plane, you will be in a different place, and yet you will remain in this world. The dual nature of each individual is that he or she possesses a material body (the flesh and blood) and an aetheric body (the mind). Each of these bodies is capable of easy movement in its own world (the material and the aetheric, respectively) and can move in the other world as well.

What follows is an exercise to help you imagine your aetheric body. You will use this body to travel to some of your favorite places in the world, without your physical self leaving the place you are right now. Don't discount this exercise as "just imagination," for it is imagination that fuels mentalism.

If you find yourself getting overwhelmed, go back to the initial practices in "The Basics of Meditation and Visualization." As with the previous exercise, you may want to ask a friend to guide you through, having them read the text aloud slowly while you close your eyes and visualize.

Exercise 5: Visualizing the Aetheric Body

Go to a quiet place where you can meditate. Close your eyes, relax, and breathe, focusing on your breath. Do this for ten minutes or until you are completely relaxed. Breathing and relaxing. When you are completely relaxed, begin this exercise for your imagination:

Picture a person standing in a big, open field. That person is your mind. That person is your aetheric body. That person is you.

You find that you can move your aetheric body around quite easily. It's as easy as imagining you are somewhere else, and there you are.

Let the field around you fade away and think of one of your favorite places to be. Maybe it is a vacation spot. Maybe it is your home or the home of a friend. Picture yourself there, in a specific room or secluded spot. How clearly can you see everything? Can you recall much of this place clearly, or is the scene hazy? Look around, checking things out a bit.

(If you are reading this to your friend, pause here for a minute or so and let them wander around in their visualization, then resume with the next paragraph.)

After you've spent some time here looking around, think of another favorite place of yours. This time choose a public place, a special shop or restaurant you like to visit. Take a little while to let the vision of your first place fade, while the new vision comes to the forefront of your thoughts. Picture yourself in this new place—construct it using your imagination—and take a look around.

Spend some time here, in this second place. If you are in a shop, look at all the displays, all those objects. If you are in a restaurant, look at the table settings, the food on the tables. Even though you are visiting this place in your mind, the things around you seem very real.

Stay here as long as you like. When you are ready to leave, let the scenery around you fade, and return to the big field where you began. Imagine the grass and trees around you. Feel the sun on your skin. Relax here. Relax.

When you are totally relaxed, return your attention to your breathing. Slowly bring your consciousness back to your physical body. It is sitting here, breathing. Think of the place where you are sitting, and carefully bring your conscious thoughts to

this place, remembering what it is like to see it. Continue to breathe slowly, and when you are ready, open your eyes and return yourself to the material world.

Congratulations, you have just taken your first trip using your aetheric body!

VISUALIZATION AND MEMORY

A good memory is essential to mentalism. The more you can remember about places and things, the better your visualizations will be. Here are some exercises to help you develop your memory and visualization skills.

Exercise 6: Observation and Memory
Try this experiment to test your powers of observation. Sit at a table that is clear but for one object. The object you choose

should be simple, without moving parts if possible. A ball, a knife, or a dish all work well for this experiment. See how long you can examine the object before your mind begins to wander. Not long? Take a breather, a few minutes, and try again. Do this until you can examine the object for at least three minutes. Use a timer to keep time.

After you have examined the object for this long, put it out of your sight but keep it in your mind. Write as many notes as you can about the object, observations that point out the physical characteristics of it. You have observed this object, examined it for three minutes. How many observations can you make? Can you fill a page with observations?

When you are satisfied with your observations—that is, when you have finished cataloging your recollections about the object—bring it back onto the table and examine it some more. Examine it for three more minutes, then return to your page, turn it over, and fill the back side with more observations.

Exercise 7: Memory of the Commonplace

In mentalism, it is often necessary to visualize commonplace items, things we see every day but often take for granted. Test your ability by conducting this simple experiment. Take a pencil and a piece of paper and, sitting *inside* your house, draw a picture of your front door as viewed from the outside. (Draw your back door if it is the one you use most often.) Don't sit in view of the door or go outside to have a look or even peek out the window. Just sit and draw the door as best you can, including every detail, from memory.

It should be easy, right? After all, you use this door each day when you leave home and again when you return. You probably take at least a quick glance at it on your way into your house. But what a mindless lot is mankind! For chances are very likely that when you have finished your diagram and gone outside to compare it against the real thing, there will be many errors in the drawing—some more grave than others—that you cannot believe found their way in.

Now make a second drawing of the door, this time sitting in front of the door and looking at it for reference. Make the drawing as detailed as you can and pay close attention to the things you left out or bungled in the first drawing. Fix them in this drawing.

The next day, sit inside again and draw your door looking neither at the door nor your previous drawings. Stop frequently as you draw, closing your eyes and picturing the door in your mind. Try to picture the door itself, not the technical lines of your previous drawings. Now compare your drawing to the first one you made yesterday. Did you make any of the same mistakes? Were there new mistakes? Compare the drawing with the actual door, then draw the door while sitting before it, like you did yesterday.

If you continue making these sets of drawings each day for two weeks, your power of visualization will develop immensely and be well on its way to helping you achieve flight to the aetheric plane.

THE MENTALISM CONNECTION

If you have read this far, you know that aether is a substance permeating all things in reality, a material that can be manipulated mentally, by force of will, to various ends, the practice of which is called mentalism. The types of feats described in the "Sculptor's Studio" visualization could be defined as telekinetic in nature (as in *telekinesis,* the ability to move material objects using thought). But telekinesis is only one of the many abilities at the mentalist's disposal.

This book will instruct aspirants in three of the mentalist's most common uses of aether, namely psychisms, astral projection, and spiritism. An introduction to each of these disciplines is offered here. Throughout this book we will explore each in detail.

Psychisms

Humans perceive the world around them with five senses: sight, hearing, touch, smell, and taste. Mentalists share these senses with untrained (also called "mundane") humans, but whereas mundanes are limited to their everyday range of sense—seeing only the things in front of them, hearing only the sounds within earshot—mentalists can perceive at a much greater distance, depending upon their level of mastery. Clairvoyance (remote viewing) and clairaudience (remote hearing) are the most common types of remote sensing, but many mentalists develop remote senses of taste, touch, and smell.

Have you ever tried to guess the number of fingers a friend was concealing behind his or her back? Chances are that you could not correctly guess the number, because you couldn't see your friend's hand. Wouldn't it amaze both you and your friend if you could guess the number not once, but *ten consecutive times?* A well-developed sense of clairvoyance makes this feat not only possible, *but likely.*

By using aether in various ways, mentalists can perform astonishing psychic feats. Mentalists develop their psychisms through practice with Zener cards and daily work with meditation and visualization. Mental powers like extrasensory perception (ESP), telekinesis, and mind reading all come from the aetheric plane.

Astral Projection

The aetheric plane is not a mere static, duplicate universe of our own. It is an active, changing place of great possibility. Things impossible in the material world are commonplace in the aether.

By expelling and condensing a portion of his or her own aether, a mentalist creates an aetheric, or astral, body that can move about independent of the physical self. This body is much like the aetheric body that you visualized in the earlier exercise. Using an astral body, the mentalist can travel to places that are inaccessible or dangerous to the physical body. Who needs a spaceship when you can travel to the moon without help from anything but your own mind?

Astral projection is perhaps the most dynamic use of aether. Mentalists can use astral projection to dive to the bottom of the ocean or to fly to the next star. Practicing astral projection takes much work and involves complex visualizations, but the freedom that comes with mastery of this study is without equal.

Other uses of astral projection combine with psychisms, enabling clairvoyance, telekinesis, teleportation, and other stupendous feats.

Spiritism

Have you ever wondered what it would be like to talk to the spirits of those who have died? Perhaps you have attended a séance or used a Ouija board to attempt such a communication. What happened when you did?

It is possible to contact the spirits of the dead via the aetheric plane. Mentalists tap into the realm of the dead during individual and group séances. This study is called spiritism and is a highly controversial topic among mentalists and mundanes alike.

The beings you contact in the spirit world are made of the same material that moves the planchette across your Ouija board or that settles your tea leaves at the bottom of your cup. That material is aether. The belief held by many mentalists—that as our souls, when disembodied, subsequently inhabit the spirit world and can be contacted by means of mentalism, so then our souls themselves are constructed of aether—has caused no end of debate.

But the disembodied spirits of the dead are not the only aetheric beings available for conversation by means of spiritism. Other aetherics dwell or travel on the aetheric plane as well, be they the aetheric aspects of mentalists practicing astral projection, or manifestations of powerful thought and emotion that have taken on an independent, rudimentary existence (such as poltergeists), or even the secret, invisible masters who have dwelt exclusively on the aetheric plane for all eternity, guiding and mentoring aspirants and accomplished mentalists alike. You will learn to communicate with them all.

Each of these disciplines has a distinct set of regimens to be followed for best results. Future lessons will be devoted to astral projection, spiritism, and psychism.

MIND IS MATTER, MATTER IS MIND

If the discussions in this lesson have planted but two thoughts in your mind, the author hopes they are that all of creation is made of a material called aether and that practitioners of mentalism may hope to manipulate aether at will. These concepts form the foundation of mentalism.

Meditate frequently, remembering to focus on your breath. This practice will help you relax and think more deeply about the nature of aether and the aetheric plane. If you spend a small amount of time each day—as little as half an hour—pondering the ramifications of your knowledge of aether, you will strengthen your capacity for mentalism in what seems like no time at all.

LETTERS FROM ASPIRANTS

Dear Editor,

Why do you insist on the "ae" spelling of aether? Isn't that a bit antiquated?

—D. A., San Francisco, Calif.

I chose the "ae" beginning for the word because I wanted to differentiate these lessons from other theories and for the substance to be recognizably different from the vapor ether, which no doubt deserves its own course of study, judging from the response I've received from ether enthusiasts. The spelling is also a nod to my predecessors from the nineteenth and eighteenth centuries, who wrote in a time that encouraged ligatures like the æ combination.

Dear Editor,
I have a concern. If truly everyone has the potential for mentalism, then perhaps this power might be used by bad people. Is mentalism used to harm others?
—O. S., Iowa City, Iowa

Mentalism can be used to harm others, but happily, it rarely is. Like all studies and practices, our ethics in mentalism mirror our everyday ethics. So if I am a basically "good" person, one who spends time helping others and not harming them, then my use of mentalism will reflect that. On the other hand, if I am "bad," I will likely use mentalism to the detriment of mankind. Consider this, though: There are so many ways to hurt someone else that take little or no effort at all, unlike mentalism. If someone studies mentalism for his own personal development, he is taking time and energy away from all the other things he could be doing. Spiteful or vengeful thought detracts from the learning. The skilled mentalist is one who can clear his mind of all other thoughts, good or ill, and focus on aether.

Dear Editor,
Can animals manipulate aether? Can plants?
—N. H., Cleveland Heights, Ohio

The thought processes of most animals are too basic for aetheric work, which is not to say there aren't instances of mentalism in animals. Bouts of strong emotion can trigger mentalism in animals just as in humans. Plants, by and large, think too slowly for humans to measure. They are undoubtedly manipulators of aether, but the effects are too subtle for us to notice. Ancient material beings like the redwood tree and the Galapagos tortoise are potent mentalists in their kingdoms of Vegetable and Animal.

Dear Editor,
What happens to old thoughts and emotions on the aetheric plane?
—D. I., Boston, Mass.

Thoughts in the aether age as they do in your mind, eventually dissipating and disappearing. Stronger thoughts last longer in the aether, though, as is evidenced by the existence of vapors (a being described in this book's aetheric bestiary). All moments in history, including the aetheric counterparts to emotions, thoughts, and objects, are cataloged in the Akashic Record, a kind of library of aetheric history. The Record is accessible from the astral world and is a very powerful tool in mentalism, albeit one that can be used for irreparable harm.

Dear Editor,
What happens to an aetheric double when its material counterpart dies?
—T. R., Portland, Oreg.

I'll make no attempt to skirt the issue of the afterlife—it's as prickly a subject among mentalists as it is among the rest of humanity. Theories of the afterlife vary from place to place and religion to religion. The soul and the aetheric body can be thought of as one and the same. The aetheric body lives on the aetheric plane during the lifetime of its material body and remains there after death. This "aetheric survival" is the benefit of consciousness of our nature as sentient beings. The same can't be said of the chair you're sitting in or the car you drive. They're both has-beens in the aether as soon as they're destroyed in the material world. Souls in the aether wait around for a time after death, until their next material form is ready for inhabitation. At that point they join with the material world once again and resume their dual nature in the material and the aetheric.

FIAT LUX

LESSON TWO.
AETHERIC BEINGS

*The Aetheric Plane, Its Worlds and Vibrations—The Astral World—
The Elemental World—The Elysian World, or Elysium—An
Introduction to Vibrational Theory—All Is Aether—Below and above
the Material—Elemental Vibration—Perception and Reality in the
Aether—Inky Flares—An Aetheric Bestiary—Animal Spirits—Astral
Hounds—Departed Spirits—Devas—The Dweller on the Threshold—
Elementals (Nature Spirits)—Elementals (Thought-Forms)—
False Gods—Gestalts—Ghosts—Ghost Stars—Lost Souls—
Manifested Spirits—Phantoms (Plant and Object Doubles)—
Poltergeists—Projected Astral Bodies of Mentalists—
Revenants—Secret Masters—Star Guides—Vapors—Wraiths*

*"It is absurd asking me to behave myself," he answered,
looking round in astonishment at the pretty little girl who had
ventured to address him, "quite absurd. I must rattle my chains,
and groan through keyholes, and walk about at night, if that is
what you mean. It is my only reason for existing."*
—OSCAR WILDE, *The Canterville Ghost*

IN YOUR TRAVELS IN THE AETHER, you will encounter a number
of interesting intelligences. These creatures will help or hinder
your cause, each according to its nature.

Presented here in field guide form are listings for twenty-one beings that may be encountered in the astral, elemental, and elysian worlds. Although we have not yet devoted individual lessons to these realms, a brief note on each can be found in the essay directly following this introduction.

No aetheric bestiary can ever be comprehensive, due to the infinite number of realities created by mentalists the world over. Keep in mind that the listings of aetheric beings in this lesson are merely composite accounts of the creatures and forces as they have been encountered in the past. Your own experiences with the same beings may be markedly different. It is hoped that this guide will give you a glimpse of some of the most common intelligences you may encounter in your experiences with aether and provide you with a framework for the classification of aetheric beings no one has yet encountered.

THE AETHERIC PLANE, ITS WORLDS AND VIBRATIONS

The aetheric plane encompasses all of reality. For most people on earth, reality seems to be bound by the limits of their material surroundings. This need not be the case. For with knowledge of aether, there are many worlds to discover and explore. As we have already discussed the aetheric plane in detail, outlining its functions and qualities, you no doubt by now understand that the aetheric world is a separate place from the world we call home, and yet it is the only true world there is.

When you visualized your aetheric body in the previous lesson, you went on a journey in your imagination. Soon you will be able to take similar trips in worlds not far removed from the material world, realms linked to us by aether. These worlds will be referred to throughout your aetheric training, so it is important that you are able to tell the difference between them. Here is a set of brief descriptions of each of the worlds we will discuss. The facts below should give you an idea of how the planes differ and of the native environments of the intelligences described in the aetheric bestiary presented later in this lesson.

The Astral World

Like the aetheric plane itself, the astral world appears at times to be made of light. Other times it seems very similar to the material world. The astral world is a conduit, a four-dimensional highway that allows us free passage to other parts of the material world and also to Elysium. Vibrationally, the astral world is closest to our own world and is the most easily accessible.

Through a slight shift in consciousness, usually attained through meditation, a person can alter the vibrational frequency of his or her body and travel to the astral world. This is called astral projection.

People sometimes visit the astral world unintentionally, spontaneously projecting their astral body. This happens most often during sleep or in the hypnagogic state between wakefulness and sleep. Some theorists believe that dreams are actually astral travels. While a trip to the astral world may seem dreamlike, your author does not endorse the idea that dreams and astral projection are one and the same.

The Elemental World

On earth, the substances we will call "elemental" fall under the classification of philosopher Empedocles of Agrigentum, Sicily (495–435 BCE), who postulated that all material things were combinations of four basic substances—fire, air, water, and earth—which he called elements.

Empedocles's elements are crucial to many belief systems, including Hermeticism and earth religions. Perhaps the combined beliefs of these systems' practitioners created the elemental world, or perhaps it has always existed and created earthly faith to sustain itself. Such is the power of belief.

As you progress in your aetheric studies, you may want to travel to the elemental world. It is divided into four kingdoms of equal size, one for each of the elements. To say the kingdoms are harsh environments is the understatement of a lifetime. Major portions of each elemental kingdom are composed solely of the purest form of its element. A trip to the earth plane, for example, could reveal nothing but solid, stonelike material extending as far as one's imagination can interpret. This singularity quickly disorients the mind and makes movement difficult. Other areas within each kingdom are made of simple elemental combinations, resulting in realms of steam, for example, or of dust. While advanced students of mentalism are encouraged to visit the elemental kingdoms, beginners should keep their distance. The exercise provided later in this lesson will give you a taste of the vibration of the element of earth without putting you in harm's way.

The elemental world is home to the elementals, nature spirits who visit the material plane to carry out duties in the name of fire, air, water, or earth.

The Elysian World, or Elysium

The elysian world, also called Elysium, is the most unknowable of all the aetheric worlds, for it is the furthest removed from our own material home. It is the resting place of those spirits finally free, the hallowed realm of souls unbound from obligations to the material world, or to any other, for that matter. For this and other reasons, travel to Elysium is most dangerous and therefore the least documented.

The spirits of the forever dead inhabit Elysium. No one who "lives" in this place awaits reincarnation, resurrection, or the like. Their eternal cycles are at an end. Elysium is also home to the

Greek pantheon and all of the sylvan creatures below the gods—centaurs, fauns, nymphs, and the rest. In this place, these beings are similar in appearance and function to the characters described in the Greek myths. If you are fortunate enough to meet them, you will recognize them at once, but you may find them subtly different from what you'd expect.

Even the most carefully plotted trip to Elysium is subject to the powerful forces that guard the place. A Lethean field exists on the near side of the elysian frequency. This vibration, named after the River Lethe in Dante's *Divine Comedy,* causes rapid decay in the short- and long-term memory functions of the human brain, often to the point where people remember nothing of their time in Elysium. Intense study of the nature of the elysian world is, in the opinion of this author, a foolhardy undertaking for mentalists of less than two decades' experience.

AN INTRODUCTION TO VIBRATIONAL THEORY

All Is Aether

The differences between the material, astral, elemental, and elysian planes are chiefly vibrational. Each of the worlds is made of aether, albeit aether vibrating within a frequency unique to that world. When you contact any of the other worlds, your aetheric body is vibrating within a range distinct from its usual rate, the one that keeps us rooted in the material world. These subtle differences in vibration allow us to see beyond the material world and into the aether.

As you can see from the title of this lesson, you are about to learn of the intelligences you will encounter in your studies of mentalism. It is a bit of a misleading term, "aetheric beings," because no matter where you go, in this world or another, you are always in the aether. Truth be told, we are all aetheric beings. The difference between us is in which vibrational range we primarily dwell.

You are familiar with the beings to be found within the material-world vibration, as you yourself are such a creature. Plants, animals, insects, and microbes share this world, too. The intelligences that exist in the astral, elemental, and elysian worlds do so at the specific frequencies unique to that plane. In this way, beings indigenous to the astral world will never encounter beings in the elemental world without the use of mentalism, and vice versa. Mentalists, however, truly have the best of all worlds, as they can "tune" their bodies to the frequencies of any of the other worlds, if only for a short while.

Despite the inability of most aetheric beings to shift vibrational frequency from one world to the next, some aetherics visit the material world. The material plane acts as a sort of interplanar meetinghouse, and here elementals, elysians, and astralites can find one another. Certain high-level intelligences, such as the select beings known as the secret masters, are exempt from such restrictions and can move among all the worlds effortlessly.

The chart provided here simplifies and compares the vibrational ranges within the aether, showing how they correspond with each world. Think of it as a map of the aetheric plane that shows not necessarily the distance but rather the terrain one must traverse to get from one place to another. Notice that the material world, the place where we live our everyday lives, is situated between the lower astral and the elemental worlds. In our day-to-day life, each of us vibrates physically at a frequency within the range for the material world. If we didn't, we would cease to exist here.

No frequencies are listed on this chart, as mankind has no instruments to measure the vibrations outside the material world

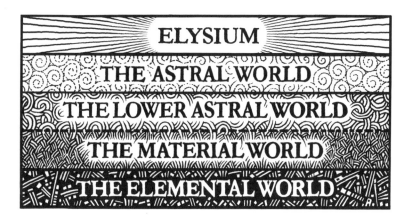

and thus no way to quantify them. Until we do, we must be content to say that the higher a world is placed on the chart, the higher (or faster) the frequency associated with that world. Think of each world as a state of consciousness, or a state of mind, if you will. This will help you understand not only the relationship between thought and place but also the relationship between state of mind and state of being.

Below and above the Material

Look at the chart. You'll notice right away that the elemental world resides below the material, vibrating at a lower frequency than you or I do. Just as the astral world is experienced at a higher, finer vibration, the elemental world is visited by tuning the mind and body down (to a lower vibration).

The border between the material and lower astral frequencies is the one most often explored by humans. The barrier between these two worlds is more porous than the boundaries between other worlds in the aether. The lower astral world is where rudimentary astral projection takes place and matches the vibration of hypnosis subjects. It is the gateway to the higher worlds of the astral and elysian.

The lower astral frequency is home to spirits of the human dead who have unfinished business on earth. Spirits still connected to their possessions or to mortal life on earth dwell within this frequency range and are called revenants. We can communicate more effectively with revenants and other spirits when we vibrate at a frequency similar to their own. This is commonly achieved through meditation.

Some humans in the material world vibrate naturally near the high or low end of the material frequency range. Their existence is distinct from that of those in the middle, and they are often recognizably different. Early cultures recognized such men and women as shamans and went to them for spiritual advice. Today, high- and low-vibration humans have great potential for mentalism. In the best of cases, high or low vibrators are blessed with superior levels of intelligence and intuition, sensing things others do not. In the worst cases, the same are also sadly prone to conditions akin to schizophrenia and dementia.

Exercise 8: Elemental Vibration

In nature, we are surrounded by rocks, soil, wind, and water. It is our preoccupation with the material representation of the elements that keeps us from experiencing their subliminal antecedents in the elemental world. If you can use meditation and visualization to move from a material understanding of an elemental substance such as soil to an aetheric understanding of the same material, you will be that much closer to your preliminary travels from the material world.

Gather some soil on a plate and sit in front of it at the table, as if you were about to eat it for dinner. Without touching the stuff, do a thorough examination of the soil. Use only your senses of sight and smell and, where your senses fail you, let your imagination fill in the blanks.

What do you know about soil? What are its properties? What are its limitations? What is soil made of? What separates it from the rest of the world? If soil represents the element of earth, how is it different from a flame, a glass of water, or a breeze, each a representative of another element? Spend some time asking yourself these and other questions that come to mind.

Once you have stared intently at the soil and pondered these questions for more than five minutes, you will no doubt have already entered a sort of meditative state. Notice your breathing and let your mind focus on the soil before you. Continue your examination as you meditate, and try not to move. Soil is immobile. It rests, supports the living things above, below, and within it. Take slow, deep breaths and feel your consciousness coming closer to the nature of the soil.

Now close your eyes and meditate upon the new discoveries you've made about soil. What would it be like to be made of this stuff? Breathe, and as you do, focus your consciousness on your breath. With each breath you mentally gain more of the rich, earthy, solid qualities of the soil. Your consciousness is slowing down, coming closer to the submaterial vibration of the elemental kingdom of earth. Can you feel it?

Of course you can. Remain at this reduced vibrational frequency for a few minutes before slowly bringing your consciousness back to a normal material vibration. It is best to ease back into material consciousness, slowly envisioning your limbs and internal organs changing from rock and soil back to flesh and blood.

Once you have returned to your regular body and frame of mind, write down your thoughts regarding your elemental vibrational experience. If you like, you may send a copy of your notes to the author. Try this exercise again later and see if you notice anything new.

PERCEPTION AND REALITY
IN THE AETHER

Because all things on the aetheric plane—objects, actions, thoughts, emotions, and so on—are made of aether, relative perception of reality is profoundly important, as the thoughts of one being alter the nature of reality for all those around it.

The consensual nature of reality is valid in the material world as well, to a certain extent. Social constructs like those surrounding work, relationships, and day-to-day life corral our actions and, whether we like it or not, our thoughts and feelings. One person's words can affect our emotions, and another person's looks might put certain thoughts in your head or mine.

If provoked by external means, some thoughts are inevitable. If I say, "Don't think of pink elephants walking tightropes!" you're bound to do just the opposite. Into your thoughts sway the pachyderms on the high wire. You can't help it, because you've been given a very specific instruction *not* to do something. Your thoughts go to the topic of the sentence. There is no way to get around thinking of pink elephants walking a tightrope, or at least it is inevitable that you will think of the elephants before you think of something else. Even the act of consciously *not* thinking of pink elephants walking a tightrope fails you, because at least initially you will think of the thing you are not supposed to think of.

Just as the pink elephants are best kept out of your mind if you don't ever think of not thinking of them, so your aetheric reality is protected if you go into the aether without preconceived notions of what you'll find there. Despite all the instruction given in this book, individual interpretation is king in the aether. This book can only give you a frame of reference. Nothing is more important than your own experience.

Stray thoughts in the aether are akin to stray dogs. They can run wild just like dogs, to good and ill effect. In the aether, where appearances can mask intentions, what you see is most certainly not what you get.

"Why then an aetheric bestiary?" you might ask. It's a good question, because at first glance, this lesson looks like a natural history of the creatures of the aetheric plane. In fact, it's no such thing at all. The entries herein are provided as a framework for you, the aetheric traveler, to use to understand the roles played by the dwellers of the elemental, astral, and elysian worlds. It is not a prescriptive text that should overrule your own judgment when you encounter these creatures.

Beginning mentalists must exercise extreme caution around more powerful aetheric beings. A creature with a better grasp on aetheric theory will always have the upper hand in a meeting with a lesser mentalist. The aether is not a place for bravado and the reckless approaching of higher intelligences.

There is an initial mental shock all lesser aetheric beings experience when they come in contact with a higher aetheric. The shock feels like the sensation of thinking you're alone and suddenly finding someone quite close to you. Another feeling people have compared to aetheric shock is the sensation of being awakened while in the hypnagogic state between wakefulness and dreams. In much the same way as this type of disturbance, an aetheric shock often snaps the mentalist back to his or her material body. A lesser shock is felt upon settling at a nonmaterial frequency, but this shock doesn't usually snap your consciousness back to earth.

Scale plays a dominant role in the aether. Things can never be assumed to have the same magnitude they hold on earth. This is true because the powers of thought, emotion, and perception are so crucial to how scale manifests itself in the aether. Just as time can be distorted there, so can space. Something that seems to tower over one visitor in the aether may appear miniscule to the next. As with all things aetheric, scale is all in the mind of— and to a great degree, the minds around—the mentalist.

Exercise 9: Inky Flares

Try this experiment, which illustrates how consciousness represents itself on the aetheric plane. Fill a basin or large bowl with water. Let a single drop of blue ink fall into the water. Do you see how the ink explodes out from its initial contact point with the water, dropping down and sending blue flares in all directions? Your consciousness ribbons out similarly as you travel in the aether, influencing other consciousnesses it encounters.

Now add a single drop of red ink to the bowl, near the blue. Streams of blue and red ink now intermingle in the water, each drop exploding and arcing ribbons over and under the other. In some places the two colors of ink meet and form a third. Eventually, as the ink dissipates, the water in the basin takes on a very pale shade of the combined color of the two inks. So it is as your thoughts meet and are exchanged on the planes.

When two beings meet on any of the planes, they partake in a consensual reality, one formed by the combination of their mental abilities. This gestalt reality affects the shapes and properties of things, as well as sound, color, light, and atmospheric mood. The reality of a weaker mentalist visiting the aether will always yield to the power of a being with stronger command over aether. In this way, it is very easy for a greater mentalist to control the reality of the lesser mentalists around him or her. Beginning mentalists should exercise extreme caution around all aetheric beings, as there are many who desire nothing more than your utter destruction.

AN AETHERIC BESTIARY

In the following pages, you will be introduced to a number of intelligences that dwell in the aether. This brief bestiary is by no means comprehensive, but it does detail some of the more prominent inhabitants of the astral, elemental, and elysian worlds. The descriptions and illustrations given here are the result of interviews with mentalists who have encountered said beings and, as such, are composite views. Use these listings as a reference for your encounters with these creatures, but look for the unique qualities of individual spirits and entities. All are living beings, and all have idiosyncrasies just like you and I do.

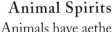 Animal Spirits

Animals have aetheric doubles just as naturally as any other thing on earth. When an animal dies, its double continues to live in the aether, manifesting to the material world when necessary.

Unlike human spirits, which may haunt sites from their life on earth in order to fulfill karmic duties, animal spirits exist mostly to aid humans, performing any of a number of functions. An animal spirit may serve as a guardian, a retriever, or a messenger. These functions are innate duties of the animal's soul, not tricks, so no training is necessary. In fact, more often than not, animal spirits aid humans without prompting from a mentalist.

The spirits of departed animals may be contacted through a formal séance or may appear spontaneously in the vision of people familiar with the animals during their lives. In the case of pets, owners are often the only mundane (nonmentalist) humans able to see the animal after death.

Visually, an animal spirit keeps the same size and shape the animal had when living, albeit with a translucent, pale-colored body. Like other ghosts, animal spirits glow slightly and are more visible in the dark than in sunlight. When an animal spirit enters a room, the vibrational frequency of the aether in the room raises slightly, increasing static electricity. Living animals in the vicinity of an animal spirit react much the same as they would if the animal were physically present (e.g., cats will often exhibit fear around dog spirits).

Animal spirits rarely continue on to Elysium after death. Those that do are often the spirits of "eternal animals"—such as the phoenix, manticore, or gryphon—that took a lesser animal's form for a period of time in the material world. Other animal spirits in Elysium act as servants to the masters and other highly evolved human spirits.

Astral Hounds

Dwelling primarily in the deep-space wildernesses of the astral world, astral hounds are highly evolved intelligences. They are solitary creatures, not at all prone to packs like material world dogs.

An astral hound manifests itself in the material world as a large black dog the size of a small horse. It may appear as any breed of large dog, but is always male. On earth, an astral hound speaks fluently in the language of any human he encounters.

Astral hounds do not come to earth unless summoned. Mentalists can summon an astral hound through a torturous regimen of meditation and fasting that lasts three days. The summoning ritual depletes the mentalist physically and mentally, so that when the hound arrives the mentalist poses little threat. A summoned hound will manifest in the form of a large black dog and sit calmly before its new master.

Once called, the hound may be assigned a task to perform in exchange for a portion of the summoning mentalist's personal aether. Astral hounds are highly efficient guardians, messengers, detectives, advisors, and killers and will not betray their summoning master even if offered a better bargain.

An astral hound can move very quickly and can dematerialize its physical body with ease to accomplish its task. This shift to its astral body allows the hound the ability to fly, teleport, or pass through walls.

The arrival of an astral hound is preceded by a chill in the immediate area, as well as a sharp metallic scent, both of which provide a bit of warning to those destined to meet this mysterious and dangerous creature.

Departed Spirits

Human afterlife is carried out in the other worlds. The exact qualifications for an assignment to the astral, elemental, or elysian world are so intricate and convoluted that no scholar could ever lay them down in printed form. One theory contradicts another, and all are faulty. This is why we have religion. Let it suffice to say that after death, a person's aetheric body leaves the material world for an existence on one of the others. Until it returns to inhabit a material form once more, by means of resurrection or reincarnation, this body is known as a departed spirit.

As you move through the worlds in your projected body, you will encounter souls who once lived in the material world. They are quite similar in appearance to astrally projected bodies, and are usually dull gray in color. For the most part these spirits will pay you no mind. The afterlife is more like a waiting room than a cocktail party, after all.

There have been cases of souls who imprison astral bodies in exchange for their freedom, so mentalists must be very cautious when they encounter a strange new soul. When this happens, the projected body is detached from its material form on earth, and the lost soul returns to earth to inhabit its new form. This type of swapping may be the basis for changeling phenomena in some cultures.

Devas

Immortal and unfathomable, devas (also called angels) are the guardians of the aether. They are ranked directly under the secret masters in the aetheric hierarchy, and they work in harmony with one another to carry out the unknowable plan of the universe. Human contact with devas is uncommon, although recently there has been a great resurgence of popular interest in angels.

Although the deva has no true visual form, it usually conforms to the beliefs of its viewer. A common form is that of a beautiful, androgynous human standing twelve feet tall. When no form is necessary, devas are invisible and undetectable. Otherwise, form follows function, and the deva can be abstract or flatly mundane, according to the need.

All is possible for the deva. Reality bends and stretches at its will. When necessary, devas can create life-forms (plant, mineral, animal, or human) from the aether to fulfill the needs of the overarching plan, including the speeding of an individual human through his or her past karma.

Devas can be invoked through concentrated meditation and visualization (in the form of prayer, if the summoner is invoking the deva through religious faith) and will arrive if the summoner's need is genuine. The most common requests of devas are those of protection and guidance. Devas will not partake in petty vengeful schemes of mortals. All works they perform are for the good of the universe.

The Dweller on the Threshold

Early on in your astral travels, you will come to a place in the aether that, although it looks new, feels very familiar. This is the Threshold.

In our earthly lives, each of us accumulates a great deal of psychic baggage. This karma weighs us down and prevents us from achieving further study of the aether. As do all things, this burden exists in a tangible form on the aetheric plane. In this form, your past exists as the Dweller, an aetheric being that haunts the Threshold and stops you dead in your tracks.

The Dweller on the Threshold exists for a sole purpose—to keep mentalists from progressing in their studies until they have resolved the baggage they bring with them. There is only one Dweller, but it looks different to each traveler. It appears as a fearsome monster to some. To others it is an insurmountable landscape or wall.

Time does not exist at the Threshold. The past and the present are the same, and the traveler must face and reconcile both before continuing on his or her path of mentalism. In one encounter or several, the traveler confronts his or her life up to that point and begins to understand his or her new life on the path of mentalism. It is a difficult process for everyone, but know that once the Dweller is overcome, your understanding of aether will deepen dramatically.

No more will be said here, so as not to taint your meeting with the Dweller, which will be as individual as you are.

Elementals (Nature Spirits)

 True elementals are nature spirits personifying the four material elements, manifesting in the form of salamanders (element of fire), sylphs (element of air), undines (element of water), or gnomes (element of earth).

When they show themselves in the material vibration, it is as shapeless masses of their element. Sometimes they appear huge, other times they are infinitesimal. Elementals do not speak human or earthly languages, and elemental speech is incomprehensible. That said, telepathic communication with an elemental is quite effective, if the mentalist is attuned to the being's low frequency vibration.

Elementals protect sites of wild nature, moving between the elemental world and the material as necessary. Elementals are never encountered in the elysian or astral worlds. Their work in the material world is carried out not from emotion or intellect, for elementals have neither. Instead they are directed by the overarching need of their element and carry out their role in the plan of the universe with a single-minded efficiency.

The kingdoms of the elemental world are unimaginably harsh environments for human travelers. There, any foreign object or being is destroyed immediately, much as our body destroys disease. Mentalists traveling to the elemental world prevent their own demise by vibrating at the exact frequency for that element. If they falter, they will either skip to an adjacent world or fall out of vibration and perish.

Smaller versions of the elementals can be called upon at a séance-type gathering or ceremony. They can be ordered telepathically to carry out small tasks, but they are unstable and unpredictable, not to mention destructive if left unattended. Nature-spirit elementals should not be confused with thought-form elementals (see the entry following).

Elementals (Thought-Forms)

 If there is one lesson to be learned from mentalism, it is that the human mind has phenomenal power over its material surroundings. The thought-form elemental is the manifestation of this tenet. Although different than spirits from the elemental world, the thought-form elemental carries out its tasks with an equal efficiency.

Thought-form elementals are created with an intense concentration session that lasts a full day. One or more mentalists focus their every attention on a particular thought or emotion. Once materialized, usually in an abstract form, the elemental needs attention to maintain its existence. This maintenance attention need not be as strong as the concentration needed to create the elemental. One mentalist may trade off with another to maintain the elemental, the two meditating in shifts.

Although elementals are mute and do not understand speech, they are highly attuned to telepathic command. The mentalist who has created the elemental may put it to work at tasks too dangerous or difficult for the mentalist's material body to perform.

The elemental grows with more thought power and shrinks and becomes unpredictable with neglect. If concentration is broken, the elemental runs astray and causes ill effects. Stray elementals will slowly shrink in power, but they should be actively dissipated through visualization by the creating mentalist so as not to cause major harm.

Thought-form elementals are not always created intentionally. Often, they are the product of an obsessive mind focused on a strong emotion such as jealousy, love, or hate. Thought-form elementals sometimes appear when two new lovers meet, spreading overwhelming goodwill, or on the frontlines of war, spreading fear. Some prisoners have spontaneously formed elementals, as have paraplegics.

False Gods

How utterly easy it is to please most humans! Money, material goods, and the attentions of others are child's play for a skilled aetheric being. Thus even minor spirits can grant many of our material wishes easily. This is why the genie is such a powerful figure in Arabian mythology but is not viewed as a god.

To put it quite frankly, the gods do not visit earth on a regular basis. They have avatars and devas to carry their messages and choose to use them the overwhelming majority of the time. This being the case, mentalists should be wary of any visit from an aetheric or material intelligence purporting to be a god, as false gods can in reality be any number of aetheric beings bent on deceiving man. As the vast majority of humanity has no regular interaction with the supernatural, even lesser aetheric beings can fool people by using their seemingly amazing abilities as proof of their divinity.

A specific type of false god is the Trickster. The Trickster archetype is common to many earthly mythologies. It arises in the Christian context as the devil, in Norse myths as Loki, and as Coyote in Native American belief. All three are separate and distinct entities, but all draw from the same primeval energy. With such a universal presence, it should come as no surprise that your aetheric path will probably cross that of the Trickster sooner or later.

Meetings with the Trickster may happen in the material world or elsewhere. While there is no good place per se to meet the Trickster, one can usually handle an encounter a little better in one's own world. True to its nature, the Trickster will appear as someone or something you think you recognize, the better to take advantage of you. How you deal with the Trickster is up to you. If mythologies worldwide have taught us anything, it's that honesty usually pays off in the end.

Gestalts

When one aetheric being's will comes in contact with another will vibrating at a similar frequency, each one shapes the other's reality to a certain extent. The ways in which reality bends to fit the conflicting wills in a given area of the aetheric plane are innumerable, but one of the most fascinating results is the creation of a gestalt.

The aetheric intelligence known as the gestalt is a sentient mass of aether that breaks away from the reality formed by two or more aetheric beings' wills. In essence, the gestalt is the illegitimate child of an unintentional aetheric union, and it combines several of the less savory attributes of thought-form elementals and poltergeists (see individual entries). Like the elemental, the gestalt requires concentration to be controlled. Like the poltergeist, it is juvenile and often quite destructive in its tendencies.

Fortunately, the average life span of a gestalt is usually only a few seconds. Those that last longer rapidly begin to pull aether toward them from other parts of the plane and in time will develop their own personalities, intellects, and emotions distinct from those of their aetheric "parents." The more developed the gestalt, the harder it is to control through mentalism.

A more scattered—but heartier—version of the gestalt is the vapor (see entry).

Ghosts

The term "ghost" encompasses several of the beings you will encounter in the aether. Into this category fall manifested spirits, revenants, wraiths, and lost souls, to name a few. Individual entries are provided elsewhere for each of these creatures.

Generally speaking, a ghost is composed of the barely noticeable aetheric remains of a material being after its soul or spirit (also called the "aetheric body") has left it. The portion of the aetheric body remaining after death sometimes becomes visible in the material world and is identified as a ghost. Even though the most famous examples of ghost encounters occur in the material world, ghosts dwell in the astral, elemental, and elysian worlds as well.

In human literature and mythology, ghosts are reminders of death, and while often frightening, their existence assures us of a world beyond that which we can see and touch.

Ghost Stars

The doubles found on the aetheric plane are by no means limited to the solar system you and I call home. Across the galaxies, billions of stars are going through the various stages of birth, life, and death. All their actions, powers, histories, and (some argue) intelligences are mirrored on the aetheric plane, which is boundless and timeless.

Ghost stars are the remaining aetheric traces of stars that have played out their lives. They remain near the site the stars held during their life cycles and communicate with other aetheric beings in the vicinity.

Some mentalists have reported success in communicating with ghost stars or at least in sensing the thoughts of these unfathomable specters. Ghost stars can be used as a kind of databank, as their memories include the entire history of the solar system they once commanded. Mentalists who have traveled to a ghost star may also use it to draw energy for further travels in the aether. Although no record exists of a mentalist using ghost star energy to journey to the edge of the universe, such a trip is theoretically possible.

Your first encounter with a ghost star will no doubt be overwhelming, as this account from Terry K., a mentalist in Philadelphia, attests:

> My first encounter with the aetheric remnants of a star came during an astral session in which I intended to travel to ancient Russia. As my astral and physical bodies separated, I could sense that something was wrong. I felt a "tugging" of my astral body, as if something were pulling me skyward.
>
> My memories are hazy, but I saw the earth vanish like a coin dropped into a well as I departed this world and hurtled, blindly, into space. In a flash I passed the moon, a place I had traveled to astrally in the past. Mars and Jupiter sped by with alarming alacrity.
>
> I'm not an astronomer, so I have no idea which part of space I was in when I finally stopped nearly an hour later. Somehow I knew I was near the resting place of a dead star. There was no light around, but

there was no black hole either, just an unimaginable material emptiness filled with a massive shrieking sound. I stayed there for about twenty minues, just floating in space and experiencing the sound.

The tugging sensation began again, only this time it was tugging me back toward earth. I let it happen, and I snapped back much faster than I had come. The trip home took about half an hour. Even though I was traveling fast, there wasn't any jarring return into my physical body.

Lost Souls

A lost soul is an aetheric body that has departed completely or nearly completely from the material body without killing it. The material body continues to live but is markedly impaired. In some cases the person falls into a coma. Other cases find the person sleeping most of the time, reacting dully or mechanically to stimulus when awake.

It is unclear why an aetheric body would leave its material host and whether or not it is a voluntary action. Sometimes the split can be traced to a serious injury, a near-death experience, or a traumatic psychic shock. In these cases, it is feasible to conclude that the aetheric body leapt to soon, thinking death was inevitable.

Lost souls can be found wandering the aether without purpose and are not very useful for much of anything. They are usually just as impaired and confused as their material counterparts. Lost souls can be coaxed back to the material world by a skilled spiritist, but sometimes the soul holds to the idea that it is supposed to be dead and puts up resistance to the reintegration.

It is important to return a lost soul to its material body as soon as possible, as the inert physical body may be mistaken for dead and destroyed.

Manifested Spirits

Spiritism is the art of contacting and communicating with the dead—more specifically, the departed aetheric bodies (or spirits) of the once living. Individually or in a group, mentalists attune their consciousness to the vibration of one of the other worlds and project a sense of warmth and openness, hoping to attract the attentions of one or more spirits. This practice is known as a séance and is a useful tool for discovering information about the aether or communicating with loved ones lost from the material world.

The beings who answer the call of the séance and manifest themselves in the material world do not always have the best interests of the mentalists at heart. Even though a loving feeling is required to attract the attention of spirits, the spirits who arrive aren't necessarily the spirits you'd hope for.

In fact, the spirits most likely to answer the call are those still attached to the material world in some way. The lower astral world—which is nearest to the material—is the home of all sorts of spirits with unfinished business on earth. The souls of murderers and their victims, the greedy, the vengeful, and the spiteful all fall into this category. Their karma has not been resolved properly, and they reside near the material vibration in hopes that someone will come to their aid. Do not fall victim to the manipulations of these spirits.

Just as a shout reaches those nearest us first, even if we are shouting to a friend much farther away, calls into the aether reach our nearest, but not necessarily our dearest, aetheric neighbors. All the same, the séance remains a valuable tool for information gathering and communion. It is best left in the hands of trained individuals.

Phantoms (Plant and Object Doubles)

 Aetheric doubles are not limited to living beings—not in the slightest. The aetheric counterparts of inanimate objects are called phantoms.

The Egyptians and other early civilizations believed in phantoms to the point of burying food and tools with the dead, in hopes that the aetheric doubles of everyday items would aid the spirits in the next world. It makes sense for us all, really. Think of the material objects that define your existence. We all form bonds with nonliving things at a very early age, the toys of childhood being the first.

Objects give us comfort and focus in our lives and help us define ourselves. Do you have a hobby? If your hobby is woodworking, for example, you know that the tools you use are essential to the art. Could you imagine a life on this or any other plane without such objects? They are tools for imagination and bring meaning to our lives.

Mentalism teaches us that all things exist essentially in our own perception of reality. Material objects (be they tools or toys) ground us and focus our attentions in the material. The same objects exist in the aether and can be used to comparative effect there.

Phantoms of natural objects like rocks and trees are very potent touchstones on the aetheric plane. Ancient sacred sites like Stonehenge have an aetheric counterpart, a place on the aetheric plane where energy is gathered and focused. The druids of Britain worked their "magic" more in Stonehenge's aetheric counterpart than among the crude rocks and grass—no matter how splendid—of this earth.

Poltergeists

The aetheric phenomenon known as the poltergeist is a parasitic spirit that attaches itself to a person, taking personal aether and using it for its own chaotic ends.

Poltergeists are usually found in the homes of families with prepubescent or adolescent children. Children of these ages can be uncontrollable and destructive, and their aetheric selves mirror this behavior, attracting the poltergeist. Throughout adolescence, our bodies change in ways that are new and strange to us. Our aetheric bodies are changing too, and as much as we wish to, we cannot control them.

The poltergeist attaches itself to a member of the family and induces unintentional telekinesis, flinging objects and sometimes other members of the family around the house. Emotionally speaking, the poltergeist is more immature than other spirits. It cannot be reasoned with most of the time, but, like a hysterical suicide case, can be "talked down" by a skilled mentalist. Poltergeists have no physical or visible form. They are "seen" by their actions—flinging household objects around like a miniature tornado. Poltergeist episodes are usually sporadic and spread out over a number of years. If a "host" (a family member) is identified as manifesting a poltergeist, it is important not to blame him or her for the destruction, as it will only increase the frequency and severity of the episodes.

Another theory of the poltergeist phenomenon posits that the family undergoes a mass hallucination, a warping of the aether in the household, while one or more family members physically wreak havoc in the house. Once the flurry of destruction is complete, the family snaps out of the hallucination and remembers nothing of what happened, only that *something* came through the house in such a rage. Even impartial observers called to the house to observe the phenomenon fall into the fugue, remembering little about the cause of the destruction. This theory suggests a possession, perhaps by a malignant spirit or stray thought-form elemental.

Projected Astral Bodies of Mentalists

Did you know that you are among the number of creatures known as "aetheric beings"? Well, part of you is, at least. When you project aether from your material body, your form joins the ranks of the dead and living spirits haunting the planes. This knowledge should make every astral traveler feel more at home on his or her journey.

While you are in the aether, you will no doubt come across the projected bodies of other mentalists. Seeing these bodies is no more jarring than seeing another person as you walk down the street. Although faces and forms are slightly different on the aetheric plane than they are in their material manifestations, when you encounter a friend's astral body, you will recognize it at once as belonging to your friend, just as you can tell your friends apart from other people you see on the street.

Because these aetherics are manifestations of human consciousness, they follow human codes of conduct, for better or worse. Therefore, trust or distrust these aetheric mentalists as you would any other person.

Revenants

Revenants are the most common type of "ghost" described by spiritists. They are the spirits (aetheric bodies) of humans that remain attached to some place or object after death. They flicker in the space between the material and astral worlds, hovering in the lower astral frequency, occasionally bobbing down into the material vibratory range and coming into view as translucent, smoky figures. Revenants are sometimes the spirits of murderers tormented by their crimes. Other revenants are the souls of the jealous or the vengeful, beings that envy and hate the living and, as such, are very dangerous. A revenant that is so spiteful it preys on living beings is called a wraith (see individual entry).

These helpless aetherics often want to leave their place in the material world, but they can't because of a karmic debt they must resolve. They can be assisted by others in this resolution. As revenants are often driven in nature and single-minded to a fault, mentalists should indulge their ghostly pleas and help them if they wish aid from the revenant in return. Revenants are useful sources of information about the aetheric plane and the history of the place they haunt. In exchange for their release, revenants may also be "hired" to haunt a person or gather information inaccessible to the mentalist.

Revenants are the most popular type of aetheric being in literature. Nearly all ghost stories are about revenants and their plights. Oscar Wilde's story "The Canterville Ghost" takes a humorous look at one such being who requires a prayer from a young girl before his soul may be laid to rest.

Secret Masters

Mysterious, remote, aloof, supreme. All these adjectives have been used to describe the ultimate aetheric beings known as the secret masters. Rumors abound as to their true nature, but conjecture is futile. The masters exist, and that is as much as we may ever *really* know about them.

The masters command the devas (see entry) and, in doing so, the fate of the universe. They dispatch their devas to correct imbalances in the aether, deliver messages to other beings, and intervene in the karmic resolution of souls. When a master deems a message or other task too important to be trusted to one of these angelic servants, it undertakes the job itself.

Masters have appeared to humans over the course of history, often dictating to them new doctrines for life on earth and spawning new movements in aetheric thought as a result. The Great White Brotherhood and Aleister Crowley's A∴A∴ both owe their existence to such aetheric dictations.

The masters are an exception to the rule of vibrational interplanar travel. Like the most skilled mentalist, a master moves easily from place to place and world to world according to its own will. While the masters are most often encountered in the material and astral worlds, they may appear anywhere in the aether.

Star Guides

Even devas (see entry) are not infallible. Or rather, despite their devotion to the masters, devas do have minds of their own. "Willful" devas, as they are known in the parlance, are usually rewarded with obliteration by their peers. Those that escape this fate go on alone, forever banished from the company of their former league.

These disenfranchised angels are known as star guides. Freed from the strictures of the masters and the overarching plan of the universe, they follow their own path and assist mortals whose intentions are aligned with their own. Even though the Bible's Lucifer falls into this category, star guides are not necessarily evil. In fact, as a class they have never been noted as such. A star guide's ethics are often not far removed from those of the mortals it contacts, however. They tend to concern themselves with the mental and aetheric progress of humans, rather than the progress of the plan of the universe.

When speaking with a star guide, it is easy to be fooled into thinking you are communicating with a deva or even with one of the masters. In fact, star guides are responsible for many of the holy doctrines of man, and their messages are often wrongfully interpreted as the word of a god. Use your judgment (see entry for "false gods") and hope for the best.

Star guides are highly mysterious creatures, appearing only to those who can help their cause. They can appear in different forms: animals, humans, lesser deities, creatures from mythology, and ghosts and spirits are all common. Sometimes star guides make themselves known through automatic writing, precipitated letters, and other means.

Mentalists enter into a relationship with star guides at their own peril. History is full of "heretics" killed by their fellow man in the name of a god. Those who follow the advice of a star guide risk retribution from even greater powers.

Vapors

As you know by now, all of our thoughts, emotions, and actions are mirrored on the aetheric plane. When we stop thinking something or lose a feeling we once had, it stays for a period of time in the aether before dissipating. This makes the aetheric plane rich with memories, emotions, and forgotten thoughts.

Crossroads of these old notions are legion on the aetheric plane. Sometimes, when two or more of these stray thoughts meet, they combine in a strange alchemy. A new personality is born, blind and stumbling, but sentient. These personalities are the vapors.

Whereas gestalts (see entry) are formed from the active wills of two or more aetherics, vapors can form spontaneously at any time. A long-dead man's thoughts can combine with those of a living child. Napoleon's dying words might join with the emotions of Aristotle.

For the most part, vapors are harmless. They may manifest themselves in the material world as a fog, a hazy vision, a soft sound, or a slight wind. If infused with strong feelings, vapors can be harmful. The presence of wrath or hate in a vapor can cause it to seek out mortals and suffocate them, for instance. Fortunately, vapors are easily controlled and dispersed by trained mentalists.

Wraiths

Wraiths are a certain strain of revenant, intent on killing any mortals that come near their homes. Like all revenants, wraiths are attached to the material and aetheric space they inhabited in life. Wraiths are vengeful and spiteful because of ill fortune during their material life, and they cannot rest until their karmic debts are paid. The wraith phenomenon is likely responsible for the vampire legends common to cultures worldwide.

It is impossible to settle their affairs for them without supreme effort, and it is foolish to try unless absolutely necessary.

While revenants seek assistance from humans to be freed from their bonds to the material world, the wraith would rather work things out itself, using aether from a material being.

Wraiths despise the living and kill humans and other material beings trespassing into their domain by draining the aether from their bodies. This gathering of aether weakens the victim and increases the tangibility of the wraith. If a wraith collects all the aether from a victim (enough to kill the being), it materializes on the material plane to the point where it may move about and interact with material objects as easily as any person. The wraith holds its stolen aether near its form and may disperse or collect it at will, allowing feats such as flight, invisibility, and movement through small spaces such as keyholes and the narrow spaces under doors. It is in this form that the wraith is the most dangerous.

The best defense against a wraith is to remove yourself from its vicinity immediately. If you encounter a wraith in the astral world, stop projecting and return to your material body at once. Strong counter-mentalism will help against an aether drain, and is best performed while in your material body.

IN SILENTIO ET SPE

LESSON THREE.
AETHERIC EXERCISES

*"Every man takes the limits of his own field of vision
for the limits of the world. This is an error of the intellect
as inevitable as that error of the eye which lets us
fancy that on the horizon heaven and earth meet."*
—ARTHUR SCHOPENHAUER, *Studies in Pessimism*

SO FAR WE HAVE EXPLORED the nature of the aetheric plane and
its inhabitants. "Aetheric Exercises" takes a look inward, explaining the way in which aether and the mentalist interact.

This lesson offers step-by-step instruction for those who
wish to perform their first feats of mentalism in the aether. The
lower astral world serves as the staging area for these feats, and

the initial exercise in this lesson explains how to get there and back.

Our own bodies contain the tools we need to step into the aether. Each of us possesses ten distinct centers of psychic energy. These centers are called "aetheric links" and correspond with parts of our physical bodies, including hands, eyes, and feet. Just as we interact with the material world using the parts of our material bodies, so do we experience and move about in the aether using our aetheric links. The portion of this lesson titled "The Body's Aetheric Links" introduces you to these points in your own body, outlining the purpose of each.

The centerpiece of this lesson is a very important section outlining twelve daily exercises for the aspiring mentalist. Dubbed "the aetheric dozen," these exercises strengthen the body's ties between the aetheric and the material worlds. With regular practice of these simple techniques your understanding of the aether will increase exponentially.

Also introduced in this lesson are rudimentary experiments in psychisms, those mental feats skilled mentalists perform as second nature. Through practice and concentration, you will learn to perform simple feats of clairvoyance (sensing faraway places), telepathy (speaking and hearing using thought), and telekinesis (moving objects with thought).

Exercise 10: Entering the Lower Astral Vibration

Here is an exercise that is absolutely vital to your progression in mentalism. This technique brings the vibration of your consciousness to that of the lower astral world, which is the theater for basic feats of mentalism. It is the initial exercise you must perform before any others in this lesson. If you have performed the exercise in elemental vibration outlined in "Aetheric Beings," then this exercise in astral vibration should come easily to you, because the two practices are very similar.

Like the elemental vibration exercise, the astral vibration exercise alters your mind's vibration to a frequency zone adjacent to your natural vibratory range in the material world. The elemental world exists in a lower frequency than the material world, so when you were in the elemental world you *decreased* your mind's vibration to reach a frequency somewhere in the elemental range. With the exercise outlined here, you will *increase* your mind's vibration considerably, raising it to the higher frequency range of the lower astral world.

This exercise should be performed in the same place you've been meditating since beginning your aetheric studies. If you can, you should open a window in the room to let in a slight breeze. If this is impossible, use a fan. Any fan will do, but the quieter the better, as you don't want to be distracted by mechanical noises during your meditation.

Your meditations thus far have focused mainly on your breath. This is not by chance. Breath and air itself are perfect metaphors for aether. Air is something that cannot be seen, but it can convey scents and light gasses such as smoke. In the same way, aether can be imbued with properties. In this exercise you will use your breath and the air around you to achieve a nonmaterial vibration, tuning your consciousness to a frequency within the range just above the threshold of the material world, the realm of the lower astral.

Stand in a part of the room that is receiving a direct breeze. Close your eyes and begin your meditation, focusing on your breath. Relax, breathe slowly and deliberately, and let your thoughts settle on the inhalation and exhalation of air. Do this until you are completely relaxed and find that your mind stays fully focused on your breath.

Now let your attention wander to the breeze that's moving through the room. In the astral world, everything you encounter appears to be in a state somewhere between a solid and a gas.

The forms and consistencies of things change depending on how you (and others around you) think of them.

Notice the breeze as in touches your skin or moves your clothing. Do not think of the breeze as a breeze but rather as a continuous wave of blue liquid. Don't worry, you will not drown—you can breathe this liquid. Things like this are possible in the aether. The wave washes around you, above you, and below you. You are floating still in the center of a sea of this liquid. As you breathe, it enters and exits your lungs. It is a special fluid. It makes you more alert and energetic than you usually are.

Continue to breathe at a normal rate, even though the feeling you get from the wave is exhilarating. The liquid is washing over you and entering your lungs, and your body loves the sensation. You notice that not only is your skin tingling, but the insides of your lungs are tingling too as they soak in the energy. It's a feeling that slowly but steadily spreads both inward from the surface of your skin and outward from the insides of your lungs, until your whole body is positively alive and glowing with energy.

This sensation is the result of a subtle shift in vibration. The wave you are in is made of pure aether. It is the aether of the lower astral world, and the moment the energetic feeling finally takes over your entire body is the same moment that you step mentally into the astral world. This realization can sometimes be shocking—so much so that you might be jolted out of your meditation. Do not let this happen. Instead, remember that you are always in complete control of your mind and your body and that you can come back to the material world any time you please.

Rest in this new vibration for at least a minute. Notice how this new sensation makes you feel. From here you may go on to perform any of the other exercises in this lesson. You should also try this vibration as a starting point for experimentation with other exercises from this book. Do whatever you please—it is your mind and your body, after all.

Unless for some reason you are shocked out of the astral world and back into the material (which is jarring and never advised, although most times it cannot be helped), you should try to ease your consciousness back to its normal vibration. Coming down from the lower astral vibration is no more difficult than going up; it is merely a matter of reverting your attention back to the material side of the astral border. Do this slowly. With each inhalation, visualize your body collecting a portion of your astral energy in your lungs. As you exhale, this portion exits through your mouth and flows back into the wave of blue liquid. Keep inhaling (collecting energy from your body) and exhaling (sending it forth) until your mind returns to its familiar material-world vibratory frequency. Let the wave of blue liquid shift slowly back into an earthly breeze, and let your mind come back to earthly thoughts.

All this will become much easier with practice.

THE BODY'S AETHERIC LINKS

Without complete use of our hands, feet, eyes, and other parts of our bodies, life in the material world can be challenging. This is also true of life on the aetheric plane. Concentrated vortices of energy in vital parts of our aetheric body serve as our aetheric hands, feet, eyes, and so on, and they allow us to move and interact with others in the aether. These vortices are called "aetheric links," and in this essay we will explore each of them.

The aetheric links are in many ways similar to the chakras described in Eastern mysticism. In fact, some of the links exist in the same place in our bodies as the chakras. Like the chakras, the links are centers of vital energy that serve to collect and distribute aetheric energy. In mentalism, the functions of the links can be very dynamic, freeing our aetheric bodies for astral flight and allowing us to perform psychisms such as mind reading and telekinesis.

There are ten aetheric links in the human body. The uppermost link is located in the center of the forehead. There are two more aetheric links in the head, one in each eye. Three aetheric links are in the human torso—one in the center of the chest, another just behind the navel, and another within the sex organs. The final four aetheric links are located in the hands and feet.

Each aetheric link is infinitesimally small, occupying a space no larger than the tiniest point imaginable. But as you know, size matters little in the aether, and, in fact, sometimes the smallest things have the most potential for power.

In thinking of each aetheric link, imagine a narrow cone with its flat part flush to the surface of your skin and tapering to a point within your body. This helps you to visualize the aether flowing between each link and the outside world. In reality, though, each aetheric link is an exact point of aether inside you, with an influence radiating outward in all directions.

Just as your material body uses its different parts to perform different tasks, so your aetheric body uses each link for a specific set of purposes. Here is a breakdown of the aptitudes of each aetheric link. Use the diagram to pinpoint the location of the aetheric links on your own body.

The Forehead Link

The forehead link is the one used to project your will upon the aether directly around you and is used in shor-range (also called "local") feats of telekinesis, telepathy, and other psychisms. It is also the link by which we lead our aetheric bodies through the aether, much as we lead an animal on a leash. Other psychic systems have called this link "the third eye."

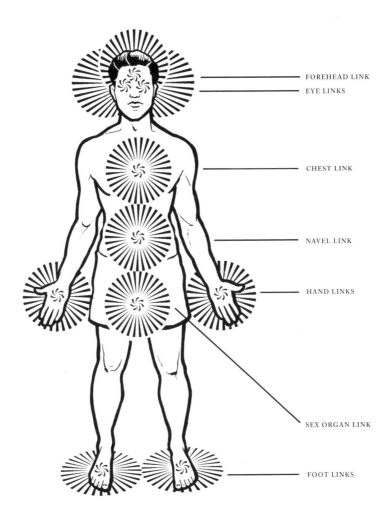

FOREHEAD LINK

EYE LINKS

CHEST LINK

NAVEL LINK

HAND LINKS

SEX ORGAN LINK

FOOT LINKS

The Eye Links

The aetheric links in our eyes are arguably the most useful when performing mentalism, as they are the links through which all our senses—not just sight but all the others as well—operate. The eye links are used to visualize the aetheric plane and provide help with all related visualization techniques, such as the solidification and transformation of aether.

The Chest Link

Astral projection is one of the most marvelous feats of the mentalist, and it is performed by using the aetheric chest link. Personal aether is expelled from this link—which is nestled behind the center of the sternum—to form astral bodies that may travel independently in the aether. The chest link draws these forms back into the aetheric body when their journeys are at their end.

The Navel Link

Resting just behind the navel, this aetheric link serves a similar function to the stomach, taking aether of one sort and dividing and transforming it into something more useful for the aetheric body. The navel receives the mentalist's personal aether from the sex organ link. It also collects external aether from the hand links.

The Sex Organ Link

The sex organ link concerns itself chiefly with the collection and concentration of personal aether from within the body. It gathers aether and prepares it for use by all the other links. This link is located just above the testes of the male mentalist and within the uterus of the female.

The Hand Links

The hand links are the points from which mental influence can extend the furthest into the aether. They are located just inside the flesh of the center of each palm and are used in long-range (or "distant") feats of psychism, much as the forehead link is used for more localized feats. Hand links are also used to draw external aether to the mentalist for use by the other aetheric links.

The Foot Links

These links are located just under the skin of the center of the soles of each foot. Their function is to ground the aetheric body partially in the material world, such that no matter what may happen during an aetheric session, the aetheric body can always find its way home.

Exercise 11: Activating the Aetheric Links

Here is an experiment that helps you attune your consciousness to your aetheric links. Begin with a ten-minute breathing meditation to relax yourself. Once you have relaxed completely, focus your thoughts on your forehead. Breathe in slowly, and as you do, visualize a rapidly swirling sphere of blue light floating inside your head, just behind your forehead, like a tiny ball of blue fire in your brain. It glows brighter when you breathe in, as if you were drawing air across a wood fire. Between breaths the sphere glows steadily and continues to swirl. As you breathe out, it burns brighter still.

After concentrating on your forehead link for a minute or so, move your concentration to your chest, imagining another blue sphere behind your breastbone. Concentrate on it as you did on your forehead link, remembering to visualize it surging with light with each breath, be it in or out.

Continue such visualizations with the navel and sex organ links. When you are through, return your thoughts to breathing for a few minutes.

Now it's time to activate the paired links in the eyes, feet, and hands. You can use the following techniques to increase the flow of physical and mental energy to these links. Still standing, lift up one foot and, using your thumb, massage the center of its sole for about twenty seconds. This will cause a stimulated sensation in your foot. Do the same for the other foot and for each hand. The hand links should be visualized as roiling, fiery blue spheres that exist half-inside and half-outside your hands. The feet links are similar, burning half-inside and half-outside the center of the sole of each foot. Concentrate on each pair for a minute or so, just like you have for the others.

Now close your eyes and place your index fingers on the sides of your eyeballs. Push the eyes in just a little, gently but firmly. This exercise will physically stimulate the eyes and, if done long enough, will produce psychedelic patterns that resemble the aether in all its otherworldly brilliance. Do this for less than a minute, as prolonged pushing can damage your eyes. Once you have stimulated the eye links physically, it is time to visualize them in the aether. Picture them as balls of blue flame that exist in the same place as your eyes. This will probably be a little overwhelming at first, but take your time and soon you'll have a good grasp on it.

It can be tricky, but it's vital that you're able to visualize each set of paired links as a unity in itself. When you visualize your hand links, for example, don't attempt to split your concentration between the two specific points. Just think, "hands." It's the same thing you do when using your material hands—when you want to do something with them, you can concentrate on their combined actions. In the same way, we shouldn't be limited to the use of only one aetheric hand at a time.

As you become more comfortable and skilled with your hand links, you'll come to possess a certain amount of ambidexterity. That's something most of us don't have even in our material bodies!

DAILY EXERCISES FOR MENTALISTS

You are already performing daily meditation and visualization sessions to sharpen your mental ability. These exercises are vital—please continue with them—but there is so much smore to learn about mentalism.

To become proficient with even the simplest feats of mentalism, you must practice some basic aetheric skills every day. This essay outlines twelve exercises—the aetheric dozen—aspiring mentalists should perform as a daily regimen. All these aetheric sessions should begin with the lower astral vibration exercise to put you into the proper state of mind, attuning your mind with the aether of the lower astral world.

As you advance in your studies, spend more time—up to half an hour—vibrating in the lower astral before beginning the aetheric dozen. As you become even more skilled, your meditation time will drop, as you will be able to put yourself in the proper state of mind more quickly. There are many theories as to why the most talented mentalists require little to no meditation before performing astonishing feats of mentalism. Perhaps they are so used to the altered state of mind produced by meditation that they are able to slip into it immediately, or perhaps their natural vibration has shifted toward the border of regular material-world frequency.

Exercise 12: The Aetheric Dozen

Use your regular meditation space for the aetheric dozen. This exercise will show the best results if performed at the same time every day. Illustrations for each of the steps in the aetheric dozen accompany the instructions.

Step 1. Grounding the Aetheric Body

The first step involves the foot links. It is a grounding to keep your aetheric body tied to the material body. Of all the steps you are about to learn, this is the most important one to perform properly. If the aetheric grounding is not achieved sufficiently, your aetheric body runs the risk of being permanently separated from your material body.

Stand with your feet apart at shoulder's width, per the illustration. Let your arms rest at your sides. Spread your fingers and

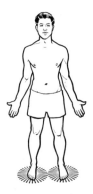

face your palms out. Imagine energy radiating from the soles of your feet. Visualize a sharp sphere of light around each of the soles of your feet and a lesser glow on the floor or ground around them. This energy is the part of your aetheric body that lives closest to the material world, grounding you in it. As long as you can visualize this strong energy being emitted from the soles of your feet, you will remain grounded in the material world and should have no fear of being lost in the aether.

GLOWING LIGHT
SURROUNDS THE
SOLES OF YOUR FEET.

Focus on this energy for at least a minute before continuing on to the next step.

Step 2. Visualizing the Aetheric Plane

In this step you use your eye links to visualize the aetheric plane around you. This step is very similar to the "Imagining the Aetheric Plane" exercise in lesson one. Using your material sight, examine the space in which you are standing, be it a room, a park, or anywhere else. Study your surroundings well enough to see the same scene in your mind's eye, or with your aetheric eyes, to be more precise.

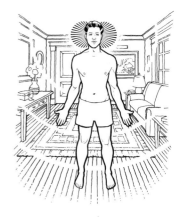

Now close your eyes and visualize your surroundings, knowing that you are seeing the aetheric double of your environment. It may be helpful to keep your eyes closed as you perform the rest of the aetheric dozen. Remain focused on the aetheric representation of your surroundings until you are comfortable in this scene, until it feels as natural or nearly as natural as the material surroundings of your everyday life. When you are ready, move on to the next step.

THE HIDDEN WORLD AROUND YOU IS NOW SEEN.

Step 3. Visualizing the Aetheric Body

Once you've visualized your portion of the aetheric plane, you'll need to visualize your own aetheric body before you can work within the aether. Form your aetheric body by using the techniques described earlier in this lesson. Focus on your forehead link before moving down the body to eye, chest, navel, sex organ, hand, and foot links. Visualize a webwork of energy connecting the links and form your aetheric body around this frame.

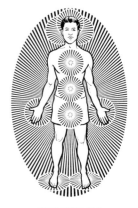

Your aetheric body occupies the exact space occupied by your material body. Performed with the right amount of concentration, this step will make you fully aware of your aetheric body. Rest for a minute or so before moving on to the next step.

YOUR BODY IS A WEBWORK OF ENERGY CONNECTED BY AETHERIC LINKS.

Step 4. Gathering Personal Aether

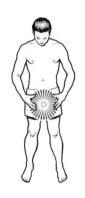

Using the sex organ link, collect an amount of personal aether already in your aetheric body. This personal aether comes from below (from the foot links) and above (the other links in your torso and head). Wisps of aether will flow freely from these places, gathering around your aetheric sex organ link.

Picture the massing aether as a pink cloud, about the size of your fist and roughly spherical. This is only a small portion of your personal aether, but it belongs to you and no one else. With it, you can performterrific feats of mentalism. We will use this small quantity of aether to conduct the remaining steps in the aetheric dozen.

PERSONAL AETHER
COLLECTS AROUND
YOUR SEX ORGAN LINK.

Step 5. Transferring Personal Aether to the Abdomen

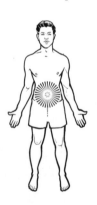

Now transfer the cloud to the navel link. Imagine it floating up a cord between your sex organ and navel links. Try to keep the cloud as cohesive as you can; don't let it stretch out too much as it travels to your abdomen. When it has risen up through your intestines and stomach to the space in your body directly behind your navel, let it stop. Rest the sphere here for at least a minute and continue to concentrate on its form, color, and consistency. When you are ready, go on to the next step.

IT MOVES UP
AN INVISIBLE
CORD TO YOUR
ABDOMEN LINK.

Step 6. Transforming Personal Aether

This step reminds us that all aether is mutable and that our minds can shape aether into anything we can imagine. Focus on the aetheric sphere now resting in your aetheric abdomen. Like your material stomach, the abdomen link can transform substances. In this step we will perform a simple transformation, one of shape and color. Meditate on the pink cloud for a few moments and then visualize it condensing to a light blue pyramid shape. This new shape should be of a slightly lesser volume (total mass) than the previous shape, as it has been concentrated a little for better use.

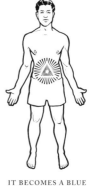

IT BECOMES A BLUE
PYRAMID OF LIGHT.

Step 7. Transferring Personal Aether to the Chest

Using the same technique as before, float your mass of personal aether up to your chest link. The chest link is just behind the center of your breastbone. Visualize the blue pyramid of aether rising slowly from your abdomen to your chest. Make sure the pyramid maintains its shape as it travels. When it is resting around your chest link, concentrate on it for a few breaths before moving to the next step, which will move the aether out of your body.

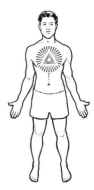

IT RISES ONCE AGAIN,
THIS TIME TO YOUR
CHEST LINK.

Step 8. Ejecting Personal Aether

Here is the first step in which you manipulate aether outside your body. The transition from controlling inner aether to controlling outer aether can be jarring, but it doesn't have to be, because the outer aether you will be working with is really just the same personal aether you've been using all along.

At this point in the aetheric dozen, you have raised the blue pyramid of personal aether to your chest link. Feel the shape in your body. It surges with light as you inhale energy into the pyramid, glows steady at the height of your breath, and then glows brighter still as you exhale.

THE PYRAMID
STREAMS FORTH
FROM YOUR CHEST.

At one of your exhales, visualize a stream of aether coming from your chest. It looks like the smoke of a cigarette being blown from a tiny hole in the center of your breastbone. This smoke comes out on each of your exhalations, and you emit it of your own accord. You have complete control over this aether.

Don't let the smoke dissipate. Instead, collect it one to two feet from your chest into the same pyramid shape as was resting inside your chest. As the shape before you grows, the shape inside you dissipates. This can be the most frightening step in the aetheric dozen and with good reason: no one is used to casually separating parts of their body from the greater whole. Why should we remain composed, in a word, as we decompose our aetheric selves? Stay calm. This split happens at a crucial point in our progress as mentalists, for as we allow a bit of ourselves to separate from our aetheric bodies, we take our first hesitant steps into the aether itself.

Step 9. Manipulating Local Aether

At this point your aetheric pyramid should be floating fully formed in the space in front of your chest.
Keep it there for a little while so you can get used to
it. It is a part of you, yet it is apart from you. Even
though this realization may come as a shock, don't
allow it to break your concentration.

MOVE AND SHAPE THE
AETHER WITH YOUR
FOREHEAD LINK.

You can manipulate the aether using your forehead aetheric link. Try it. By sending concentrated
thoughts from your forehead to the pyramid you can
make it change its shape, color, or any other properties that you can imagine. Do this a little bit if you
can, but keep it simple at first. As you repeat the
aetheric dozen each day, you will become more con-
fident in your mental abilities and will try more
complex transformations.

Your forehead link can also be used to push the
aether away from your body. Do this now, moving the blue pyramid to a distance about ten or fifteen feet away from your body.
You should also use your hand links to move the aether as it gets
further from your body. If you are performing this exercise
indoors, you may have to imagine the pyramid moving through
a wall to get it this far away. The aether will move through
walls—and anything else—easily if you are focusing your concentration on it. When the pyramid is sufficiently far away, rest
it there for a few moments before moving on to the next step.

Step 10. Manipulating Aether at a Distance

Once you've moved the aether a good distance from your body, let it hover in space around the level of the chest link from which it projected. This aether is your envoy, and it can act on your behalf anywhere on earth—and beyond for that matter. For now, let's try some simple experiments with it close to home.

You are free to manipulate your aetheric envoy however you like, giving it abilities like hearing or sight. If it has gone through a wall into the next room in your house, try to listen to conversations or ambient noise in that room.

Perhaps you would like to use your envoy as an independent "third eye" through which you can see the world. If so, it is only a matter of transferring your eyesight to this mass of aether separated from your body and floating freely in space. As with all aetheric experiments, the only thing holding you back is your own imagination.

Use your hand links to move your aetheric envoy from place to place. Use your forehead link to imbue your aetheric envoy with powers of sight, hearing, or speech. Play with your aetheric envoy, instructing it to do your will. When you are ready, bring it back to a distance no more than ten feet from your body and float it there for at least a minute before continuing.

Step 11. Drawing Aether to the Body

Now, using your hand links in the aetheric world, draw your aetheric envoy back to your body. Do not let it put up any resistance. This aether is a part of you, and it performs on your behalf. It is not a sentient being, and should it act like one, it is your duty to put it back in line. Bring your envoy closer as you breathe. It pulses brighter and draws nearer with each breath.

When the pyramid (or whatever shape your envoy is after its journeys) draws near to your body, rest it a foot or so away from your chest. You will use your chest link to draw the aether back into your body, a reverse of the process you used to emit it. Take

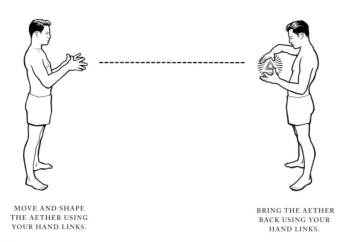

MOVE AND SHAPE
THE AETHER USING
YOUR HAND LINKS.

BRING THE AETHER
BACK USING YOUR
HAND LINKS.

your time in order to avoid shock. Bring your aetheric traveler back into your body slowly, inhaling it directly into your chest a little bit at a time. As the aetheric shape before you diminishes, you should feel a complementary shape growing within you, inside your chest.

Continue to draw in the aetheric envoy until there is no more of it outside you, and all that is inside you is gathered as a cohesive whole. Reacquaint this aether with your body, letting it glow and burn with each inhalation as you continue the meditation that keeps your consciousness on the aetheric plane. It's a complicated procedure, to be sure, but it's the type of thing you need to learn as a basis for even more complex feats.

Step 12. Distributing Personal Aether

This final step assures that the aether you've drawn into you is redistributed evenly throughout your body. The aetheric pyramid you drew in through your chest link should be floating in the same place it was before you ejected it, just behind your breastbone. Make sure it's there and that you are concentrating

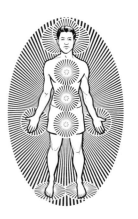

EACH OF YOUR
AETHERIC LINKS
RECEIVES ITS SHARE.

on it as intently as ever before continuing with this step—this is no time to break concentration.

When you formed the aetheric cloud in your sex organ link earlier, you did so by drawing personal aether from above and below. Now is the time to dissipate the pyramid and redistribute its aether to the whole body, concentrating especially on the body's aetheric links. Start with the foot links. Let some of the aether float away from the pyramid, like smoke off dry ice, and float down to the soles of your feet. Let it stop when it gets there.

Because you have ten aetheric links in your body, each link should receive about a one-tenth portion of the pyramid's aether. Let two such portions fall down to your feet, reducing the size of the pyramid in your chest. When your feet receive the portions, rest. Visualize your feet glowing with a bright light. The aether belonging to your feet has been redistributed.

Let another portion fall down to your sex organ link, stopping it when it gets there. When the proper amount of aether has dropped to your sex organ link, visualize a bright light around it.

Continue to distribute portions of aether to your hands, your navel, your chest, your eyes, and your forehead. Aether moves from the chest link to the eyes and forehead link like steam rising off a bowl of hot soup. As each link receives its aether, that link radiates a bright glow. When all the links are re-energized, the light spreads out to fill your body.

Soon your whole body is glowing with a bright light as the aether emits from each link to the surrounding tissues. Let the light glow brightly for a minute and then let it fade, slowly, as you return your consciousness to your breath and begin to return from your astral vibration to a material-world vibration, following the technique you learned in the beginning of this lesson. Give yourself as long as you need to reduce your vibration, and let your mind come back to earthly thoughts and earthly surroundings slowly.

When your vibration reaches its natural material frequency, open your eyes. You are back at home in the material world. Good job!

STARTER PSYCHISMS

Your work with the aetheric dozen provides an excellent foundation on which to build your psychic abilities. Supernatural feats achieved using the aether are known as psychisms.

Psychisms can be divided into two classes—passive and active. Don't be fooled into thinking that the word "passive" in this sense means "weak." Passive psychisms include many powerful phenomena you have no doubt heard of before, including clairvoyance (seeing things not physically visible), clairaudience (hearing things not physically audible), astral projection (out-of-body experiences that can include other psychic phenomena), precognition and postcognition (mental sensing of events before and after they have happened), thought reception, and mediumship (communication with aetheric beings).

Active psychisms are equally fantastic and include among their number thought transmission, telekinesis (moving objects using mental energy), psychic healing, teleportation, levitation, invisibility, and time travel.

Numerous theories exist as to the true mechanics of each of these psychisms. Obviously, given the nature of aether, there are many ways to perform a simple psychism. For the purposes of consistency, we will touch on many techniques but instruct in only a few.

Here are three exercises you should practice regularly to increase your psychic abilities. These exercises provide basic instruction in clairvoyance, thought transference and reception (also known as telepathy), and telekinesis.

Exercise 13: An Initial Exercise in Clairvoyance

Clairvoyance is also known as remote sensing. Specifically, clairvoyance pertains to the phenomenon of seeing things hidden from our direct line of physical sight. Using clairvoyance, a mentalist can see the face of a person standing behind a closed door, look around a corner in the house without physically moving, or take a (very) private tour of a closed museum or other building. These are just three examples of how clairvoyance can be used, of course. The limits you face with this and any other psychism are the exact limits of your own imagination.

You can perform some psychisms using the aetheric envoy formed in the eighth step of the aetheric dozen, "Ejecting Personal Aether." In fact, the exercise outlined here is an excellent one to incorporate into the daily regimen you've just learned, as are the exercises in telepathy and telekinesis to follow.

Try this the next time you perform the aetheric dozen: Once your aetheric envoy is formed and floating in front of your chest, it can perform simple actions in your stead. By extending certain senses and abilities to the envoy, you enable it to do things you wouldn't normally be able to do. To make a clairvoyant envoy, you must transfer a portion of your sight to it. This is simple and yet amazing. Float the envoy up to eye-level and then bring it close enough to your face that it comes in contact with your eye links. Once it is there, look through the envoy to "see things from its point of view." At this point, visualize your sight transferring to the envoy. Allow the envoy to take on sight for your consciousness. This may take more than one attempt. Once it is done, though, you will gain sight via the envoy no matter where you send it. If at first this exercise does not produce satisfying results, try it again and again until you can at least achieve rudimentary remote viewing. Sight can be transferred back to you by bringing the envoy back in contact with your eyes. Don't worry about losing the envoy. It will snap back to you immediately if you are jolted out of your meditation.

Use the envoy to explore places far from your meditation space. To lessen the shock of this dual existence, imagine that the envoy is, in fact, you and that you are traveling to these far-away places. For all intents and purposes, it *is* you. Practice this all slowly at first. There is no rush. In fact, if you do hasten your clairvoyant progress you will no doubt falter. Expect failure at first, just as toddlers should expect failure at their first attempts at walking. But like those toddlers, be sure to expect wonder as well.

Exercise 14: An Initial Exercise in Telepathy

Telepathy—the reading of thoughts—is not far removed from clairvoyance. Just as all things in the material world can be seen with material senses, so can things in the aether be seen with aetheric senses. Ride with me a distance on this train of thought: If, in fact, all things tangible and intangible are represented in palpable forms on the aetheric plane, then it is nothing at all for a person exercising aetheric sight to "see" a thought as it emanates from a person's head! This is one method of telepathy, and you must agree that it is the most straightforward. If thoughts can take shape on the aetheric plane, then they can be seen using aetheric eyes.

Develop your telepathic ability by practicing this exercise, which involves a friend. The two of you should sit across from one another at a table. One of you should enter the lower astral vibration—perhaps your friend could help you by reading aloud the astral exercise from the beginning of this lesson while you perform the meditation. Once you are vibrating in the astral range, you should notify your friend by some sort of preset signal, by dropping a hand to the table, for example, or by uttering a secret word the two of you agreed on beforehand.

Now you are aetherically awake and ready to read the aether like a book. Have your friend think a thought and think it strongly. It is important to stress that this thought should be one with a relatively powerful emotion behind it, as this will make the message much more clear to your aetheric eyes. Only you and your friend know where each other's passions lie, so no example is given for this portion of the exercise.

It's difficult to say exactly how the thought will appear when your friend thinks it. It could be seen like a picture, it could read like the front page of the newspaper, it might even be heard like a voice. What matters is not the thought's form, it's that you can perceive it using your aetheric senses.

To get a better sense of thought having shape and mass, think of it as being as tangible on the aetheric plane as a coffee cup or a shoe is in the material world. Once you see the thought floating in the aether, make a good effort to remember every detail about it. When you return to your material vibration, record the entire experience and compare notes with your friend.

Exercise 15: An Initial Exercise in Telekinesis

Telekinetic experiments follow the same basic premises as techniques for clairvoyance and telepathy, but there is a crucial difference between those exercises and this one. That is, telekinesis *crosses over* from the aetheric world to the material world, visibly affecting both at once. The practice of telekinesis is a difficult one, because it requires the mentalist to concentrate dually on two realities—the aetheric and the material.

In a successful telekinetic trial, you will use your mental energy to affect physical phenomena in the material world. It's an incredible thing to witness, to be sure, and competent practitioners of telekinesis are few and far between.

Sit at a table devoid of all objects save a piece of white typing paper and a coin. It is best to use a penny, as its color is much different than that of the paper. It is also lightweight. Trace the outline of the coin onto the paper with a pencil. This circle you have drawn represents the space the coin fills, and if your experiment is successful, the coin will move from its current space, leaving the circle behind on the paper. If you have another coin of a dark color you would like to use, make sure it is as dark as

or darker than a penny. Dimes are too light in color for this experiment (your aetheric eye might confuse them for the paper), and quarters or dollar pieces are out of the question, as they are much too heavy for beginning telekinesis.

Close your eyes and use the exercise from the beginning of this lesson to enter the lower astral vibration. Once there, activate (visualize) your forehead and hand links—these are the points of your aetheric body you will be using in telekinesis. Concentrate on each link as you do. Picture the links as sources of light, each one of them a glowing orb of aetheric energy.

Once you have activated your aetheric links, open your eyes. (You may keep your physical eyes closed if you prefer and open your aetheric eyes only. Any telekinetic force on the coin will be apparent by the circle you drew on the paper, so you need not "see" the coin move with your material-world eyes.) Focus your attention on the coin. Your hands are glowing with a supernatural light, as is your forehead. These points are the tools you will use to move the coin.

The coin is an object in material space. But it exists in the aether as well, and you are in the aether now more than ever before. Moving the physical coin with your aetheric skills is very difficult at this point in your training. Strive instead to move the *aetheric* coin that is also there before you. This will be difficult at first, because the psychological barrier between the material and aetheric worlds is very strong.

Now, using aetheric force from your hands or your forehead, move the coin. If at first this does not work, remember to focus on the aetheric coin before you. You are made of aether, the coin is made of aether, and the space between you and the coin is made of aether. When you move your aetheric hand, all the aether around it moves, including the aether of the coin. Try this and see what happens.

Amazing, no? It is nothing compared to what you have yet to learn.

ADJUSTING YOUR DAILY ROUTINE

Make no mistake: At first you will struggle to practice these exercises several times a week, let alone daily. It is important that you not let this struggle discourage you from your practice of mentalism. The goal is to slowly make mentalism and the aether a part of your conscious daily life.

In making a daily habit of the aetheric dozen, it can help tremendously to always perform the exercises at the same time of day. Morning works better for some, nightfall for others. Some prefer to visit the aetheric plane on their lunch break. Still others report that an aetheric excursion brings them closer to the twilight realm of sleep, and so they perform the exercises just before retiring to bed.

Have you got any regular daily habits? Most people do, and you would be an exception to the rule if you did not. An easy way to integrate the aetheric dozen into your life is to tie the exercises to another daily habit. Most of us shower or take a bath at the same time every day. What if you were to perform your aetheric exercises after your bath?

There is more time in the day than you think. Each of us is given the same twenty-four hours each day to do with what we wish. Before starting the daily aetheric dozen program, you may want to take a mental inventory of a usual day's activities. Take a look at yourself. Are there things you do every day that aren't really that productive or things that are even destructive? By cutting out some habits or pointless daily activities, you will free up time and energy for a new routine, like the aetheric exercises you have just learned. It is up to you to decide what is and isn't healthy in your life and make adjustments accordingly.

Even when you have made the aetheric dozen part of your daily routine, you will likely still struggle with the practice. At first the exercises will be difficult and time consuming, and they might seem like more of a bother than a help, especially if you are not seeing results right away. Don't be discouraged. Continue your practice and slowly you will see results. Just like you can't rush physical training when you are trying for a certain physique or a diet to achieve a certain body weight, you can't rush mental development. It is a slow process, but one that each day builds on the previous day's successes. Keep it up!

HEALTHY MATERIALISM

If this lesson has achieved its goal, you are now aware that the only way to mental mastery is through a daily regimen of aetheric exercises. Aspiring mentalists should know, however, that the aetheric dozen outlined herein are only half of a regular program that exercises both the mind and the body.

In addition to your daily excursions in the aether, you should also remember that physical exercise is an immense help to your growing mentalism skills. A healthy body feeds a healthy mind. If you do not already follow a regular workout, consult your doctor and ask that he or she prescribe physical activities at least as strenuous as the mental regimen you are now engaging in.

The intensity of your physical routine will be unique to you. For some people it will be as simple as a daily walk around your neighborhood. Others will be prescribed a vigorous workout requiring modern gymnastic equipment. The author of this book is not qualified to tell you what is or is not good for your physical body. Your physician's advice is important. Heed it and do not overexert yourself.

Aside from your workout, another key element in cultivating a healthy body is diet. Review your eating habits with a professional nutritionist, explaining that you are involved in a program that emphasizes both bodily and mental health. Ask for a diet outline that will give you the proper amount of vitamins and nutrients to bring your body to its peak potential. Avoid fad diets and stick to a mixed intake that includes lots of fruits and vegetables, which are excellent sources of physical and mental nutrition.

If you do these things, you will find that you have more energy to perform the aetheric dozen outlined in this lesson. Your day will stretch out before you, and you will wonder how you ever whiled it away so effortlessly. Before you know it, you will be eating well and exercising as if it were second nature, and even though it seems like a chore at first, soon you won't mind the effort it takes to lead a healthy life.

TAMQUAM ALTER IDEM

LESSON FOUR.
ASCENSION

*Internal Aether—Strengthening Internal Aether—Common
Questions about Internal Aether—Many Bodies, One Self—
The Sublime Bodies—Initial Exercises—Awake around the Block—
Getting to Know You—A Material Dissolution—A Separate Self—
Projecting the Astral Body—Ascension—Your Astral Neighborhood—
Going Higher—Psychic Residue—Aetheric Housekeeping—
Dissolution of Everyday Objects—The Dweller on
the Threshold—Crossing the Threshold—Going On*

*"It's not far, by bird, from a cloud to a man . . .
everything is transmutable into everything."*
—PAUL ELUARD, *A Toute Épreuve*

OF ALL MANKIND'S FANCIES, the dream of flight is one that
has diminished little since the days of Icarus. The advent of air
travel in the early twentieth century brought people to the skies,
but still the dream lives on in everyone's mind, including, no
doubt, yours. And it is the mind that will serve as the vehicle for
your first true experience of flight.

As a practitioner of the exercises described in these pages,
you are already well versed in the basics of aether, the universal
substance that ties all things together. Now you are about to

learn how you can use the aether to perform a singularly spectacular feat—astral projection.

Building on the aetheric dozen, the set of exercises you've just learned, you will use memory and visualization techniques that will open your eyes to an entirely new world, one made of a much finer grade of aether than the world we normally inhabit. By forming and then separating your astral body from your material form, you will achieve free movement—including flight—in this other realm, a place known as the astral world.

INTERNAL AETHER

So far you have learned much about a type of aether called internal aether. In this section we will explore the functions and limitations of this substance. Keep in mind that internal aether goes by many names. All these names mean essentially the same thing:

> internal aether
>
> personal aether
>
> the mind
>
> the consciousness
>
> the aetheric body

Internal aether is differentiated from external aether in that it is the aether that composes what you think of as your self—that is to say, your personality or consciousness. Internal aether composes your physical and aetheric bodies, your thoughts, your feelings, your memories, and your personality. In a word: you.

Your internal aether is controlled in much the same manner as your physical body. Think of this: Some of your material body's functions are subconscious or involuntary. These functions include breathing, blinking, reflexes, and other reactions and essential life processes. Other functions of your body come naturally to a grown person but are voluntary, such as walking, talking, and performing complex tasks like driving a car or cooking. Just as you control your body to do these things, so you control your internal aether to perform its functions. In fact, as you are cooking or sleeping or breathing in the material world, your aetheric body is doing the same in the aetheric world.

External aether, in contrast, is defined as all the aether that composes things that are not you. You can no doubt name a countless number of things that are not you. Right now, the things closest to you that are made of external aether are the clothes you're wearing, the air you're breathing, and the place in which you're reading this book. In fact, this book itself is made of external aether.

Exercise 16: Strengthening Internal Aether

In order to use your internal aether to its fullest potential, an aspiring mentalist must exercise his or her aetheric body (composed of internal aether) just as an athlete would exercise his or her physical body. Here is a simple exercise you can perform as part of the aetheric dozen set of exercises you learned in the last lesson.

The next time you complete the aetheric dozen—that is to say, when you have performed all the exercises and are standing with your replenished aetheric body in your practice space—do something totally mundane while your consciousness remains in the astral frequency. What are the objects in your practice space that you could pick up or use? If you have properly visualized the aetheric plane around you, then they should all look like faintly glowing doubles of the actual material objects. Keeping your mental vibration high, walk over to one of the objects and use it the way you would normally. Keep this simple at first—it is better to pick up a ball and toss it from one hand to the other than to read a book, as reading takes more of the focused concentration and reflection you need in order to keep your consciousness in the astral frequency.

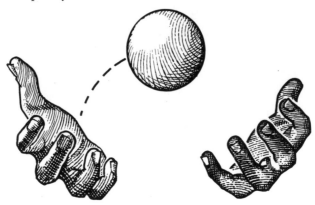

Tossing a ball, folding some laundry, eating a cracker—all these things are perfectly good to do for the purposes of this exercise. What's important to think about as you do it is not so much the activity itself but the motions your body is making to perform the activity. Your hands are moving, no doubt. Maybe your legs are too. What about your head? If you've chosen a mundane task like those listed above, you will be able to think about how your body is moving and how what you think translates directly into what you do—or rather, what is done. Because your internal aether is your consciousness, the more conscious you are of your body—its movements and functions—the stronger your internal aether becomes.

Do this exercise after your daily dozen for a few days and see if you notice anything about yourself that you didn't know before. It is not necessary to keep doing this exercise every day after that, but remember that it is there for you if you need to strengthen your consciousness of your body.

Common Questions about Internal Aether

Under what circumstances does external (or personal) aether become internal aether, and vice versa?

The answer to this question is more complicated than it appears at first glance, and, in fact, there are no hard and fast rules governing what is and is not internal aether. What are some examples of the external becoming the internal in the material world? Drinking a glass of water, smoking a cigarette, even the simple act of breathing all take outside material and incorporate it into our bodies. As aetheric beings we can take the external into ourselves in much the same way. In fact, we do it as a matter of course, for when you eat a piece of fruit in the material world, you take the fruit's aether just as you take its flesh, and both provide nourishment to your respective bodies.

Think about the penultimate exercise in the aetheric dozen, "Drawing Aether to the Body." In that exercise, you bring your aetheric envoy (internal aether sent forth from the body) back into your aetheric body. With practice, you can consciously bring external aether into your aetheric body.

Does internal aether have a personality of its own?

Yes, it does, but that personality is the same as your own. In rare cases, the personality of an individual's aether is significantly different than that of his or her material-world personality. This is usually caused by mental illness or possession by a poltergeist or an even more powerful aetheric being that commands the personality. In those instances, the internal aether is still the victim's own, even though it is no longer under his or her control.

At what rate does internal aether vibrate?

I'm so glad you asked that question, because it brings us to our next subject.

Many Bodies, One Self

Depending on its vibrational frequency, your internal aether composes one of a number of sublime bodies that exists in tandem with your material self. Most of the time your internal aether is vibrating at a rate within the material range, albeit on the aetheric plane. Our material and aetheric selves can exist simultaneously due to the existence of the aetheric plane. As you meditate and raise or lower your internal aether to other worlds within the aether, your consciousness changes from its normal material-aetheric form to one more suited to the new world it inhabits.

If you've been practicing the aetheric dozen, then you may have already made an astonishing realization: each time you have raised your mind's frequency to the astral world, your personal aether has done likewise and formed an astral body. While you practice the exercises, the astral body inhabits the same space as your physical body. In this lesson you will learn techniques for moving your astral body to other places while your physical body remains still.

The Sublime Bodies

The Elemental Body: The aetheric form known as the elemental body exists at the lowest aetheric vibration and is the most dynamic of all the sublime bodies, due to the variegated nature within the elemental vibrational frequency range. Depending on where in the elemental world your travels take you, your elemental body will become fiery, airy, watery, earthy, or a combination of the four. In some instances, the elemental body can exist in the material world.

The Material-Aetheric Body: This body is known as the "material-aetheric" body instead of just the "material body" to help you keep from confusing it with the physical body you

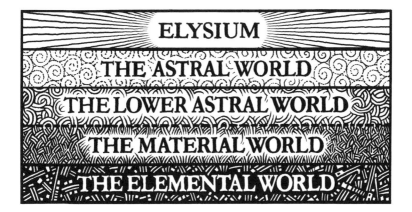

use every day in the material world. Your consciousness is in its material-aetheric form when you go about your mundane, daily affairs, not practicing mentalism or altering your mind's vibration through meditation or other means. You use your material-aetheric body when you daydream, putting yourself in places or situations that are totally imaginary.

The Astral Body: Most of the feats and techniques you will learn as a mentalist will use the astral body. The astral body is an ideal vehicle for mentalism and aether manipulation for a number of reasons. Firstly, the heightened awareness achieved through astral-vibration meditation focuses your mind sufficiently for aetheric work. Secondly, the astral world is a remarkably pliable place, so you will find it a welcoming venue for your experiments. Thirdly, the variety of beings and energies existing in the astral world provide the range of experience essential to your progress as a mentalist. There are other, lesser reasons why the astral world is ideal for mentalism, and as you perform your own studies there, you will no doubt come up with a list of your own.

The Elysian Body: The elysian body is the aetheric form your consciousness takes on once its vibration is raised past the upper limits of the astral world and the Lethean field separating the astral and elysian frequencies. At this point in your studies, Elysium is nothing but the remotest of destinations reachable in your aetheric travels, so for now we will not dwell on the functions of this sublime body.

INITIAL EXERCISES

The activities we take part in every day can also be performed in the astral world. In fact, a simple thing like a walk around your neighborhood can serve as the perfect introduction to astral projection. The material world offers many such illustrations to help you understand the aether more fully. In this section you will learn three material-world exercises that will prepare you for your initial forays into the astral world.

Exercise 17: Awake around the Block
Have you got a short route you walk on a regular basis? Perhaps you go to a store or a bus stop a few blocks from your house several times a week, or maybe you have incorporated a short stroll into your exercise program. Regular walks such as this improve your physical health. When you practice mentalism, you can perform similar walks in the astral world to improve your aetheric well-being!

Make sure the route you choose is a short one, with your farthest point no more than three blocks from your house, and try this: the next several times you go out on your walk give yourself extra time to notice the details of the world around you. Set aside a week in which you'll take your walk a few times in a much more conscious manner than usual. Take half again or twice as much time on your walk, so you can observe as much as possible. Look, listen, and smell the things around you on your way, paying extra attention to sensations you don't normally notice. Breathe deeply, getting a real feel for the air of the place. Is it sunny? Are there lots of buildings? How many trees or other plants do you pass on your walk? Are there many people around?

When you return from your walk, take some time to remember what you can of it. Retrace your steps in your mind, ideally spending as much time in recollection as you did on your stroll. Memory can be very selective. We tend to remember only certain obvious or remarkable things we see or hear. As a student of mentalism, you must remember what all your senses are telling you and the details of everything you perceive. At first you may find that you are remembering your journey as a series of more powerful sensations connected by less memorable ones. As you practice your recollections, your memory will improve, thus improving your visualizations of this trip.

Exercise 18: Getting to Know You

Here is an exercise that will help you visualize your projected astral body. Stand naked in the bathroom or any other well-lit room that has a full-length mirror in it. Examine your reflection standing about an arm's length from the mirror. You already know your body so well, because you inhabit it and use it constantly, but now you are looking at it the way you've been looking at your neighborhood in the previous exercise. Get a good sense for the proportions of your body and how you look from the side and front. Look over your shoulder or use another mirror to get a look at yourself from behind. Then close your eyes and take a few minutes to picture your reflection from each angle. Open your eyes and compare your mental image to the reality in the mirror. Do this a few times. Remember: you are trying to build a strong mental visualization of your body. This is not the time to attach any negative or positive thoughts to your body image. Try to remain as objective as possible.

Now stand very close to the mirror, almost to the point where you're so close you can't focus. Look at your face. Study its details just as you studied your body's details. A mental picture of your face is vital to beginning astral projection, so pay close attention. Now close your eyes and visualize your face. Can you see it? Concentrate on its image for a minute or so and then open your eyes to your reflection. How close is your mental picture to the real thing? Keep studying your face and picturing it in your mind until you know it well.

Step back from the mirror and see your whole body again. Begin to notice your breath. Take a few deep breaths, and on one of your inhales, close your eyes and picture your body. When you exhale, open your eyes and see your reflection. Do this several times to increase your mental familiarity with your body, and then repeat the exercise focusing on your face.

When you are through with this exercise, take a break from such introspection. Read a book or go outside. Be around other people. It will do you good and will let the things you've just learned sink in to your subconscious for recall later.

Exercise 19: A Material Dissolution

As you learned in the "Inky Flares" exercise, water is an excellent medium for illustrating the properties of the aether. In the exercise described here, you will need a (preferably transparent glass) bowl of water filled nearly to the top, a sharpened pencil, and a small box of sugar cubes.

Imagine that the bowl of water represents the room you are in. The room is filled with aether, as it always is, and you are in it. With your fingers, carefully set a sugar cube in the bottom of the bowl. Now look closely at the sugar. After a moment or two you will see the sugar beginning to dissolve. Watch as it does.

Notice how the solid cube slowly comes apart and melds with the water around it. Make note of how this particular sugar cube dissolves. Put another cube in the bowl and notice if it behaves the same way.

After you've watched these two dissolve on their own for a bit, put a third cube in the bowl. Stir the water around with your pencil, creating a whirlpool. Pay close attention. How does this movement affect the dissolution of the sugar cube? Try other things with the pencil. Flake away bits from the edges of the cube, poke directly into its center, twiddle the pencil just to the left or right of the cube and notice how the sugar comes apart when you do.

Perform these experiments again the next day, always noting how different conditions affect the dissolving sugar cube. Write down your perceptions and don't forget to keep track of them mentally as well. Try to remember the way the sugar cubes dissolved during your next meditation session.

A SEPARATE SELF

This section will guide you through the formation and separation of your astral body from your material body. Because of the importance of this exercise, aspirants are advised to read this section through at least once before following any of its instructions.

This exercise should be performed at the end of your daily aetheric session, while you are still vibrating in the astral world, and one day after performing the "Getting to Know You" exercise presented previously. It's okay to go back and repeat the mirror exercise if it's been more than a day. Remember to wait until the next day to try this exercise, though, to give your mind some rest and to be sure you can truly recall the memories.

Exercise 20: Projecting the Astral Body

Lay down on your bed or on the floor near a wall, facing the ceiling. When you are more accomplished with this technique, you can try it while standing or sitting, but for now, it's safer to try astral projection on your back, so you don't have to worry about keeping your physical body's balance.

The aetheric-material grounding you perform in the aetheric dozen involves your foot links. Your foot links continue to provide your firmest grounding while you are on your back. Put your bare feet against a wall, if possible, while you are lying down, to keep physical contact between the soles of your feet (and their respective aetheric links) and the material world.

If you have just completed the aetheric dozen, your consciousness is already vibrating in the lower astral range. Your initial astral trips will take place in this vibration. At this point your astral body occupies precisely the same space as your physical body. What we must do is transfer your consciousness outside your material form. The first step in accomplishing this is to form a very clear, very precise mental picture of your body.

Continue the deep meditation used for your aetheric exercises—focus on your breath. If it helps, think of the astral world as a deep blue wave of energy washing over you, as you have done before. Remain in this state for a minute or two before continuing.

When you are ready, shift your focus from your breath to the memory of your face in the mirror the night before. Allow yourself plenty of time to form a clear mental picture of your face, with all its details. Think deeply on it. Imagine this face floating directly above your own face, so that you are looking into a mirror image of your own visage, just like last night. The difference is that this time it is real.

Once you've established a good representation of your own face floating directly above your own, move your attention down to your chest link. From this microscopic portal in your solar plexus you must now emit a good deal of your personal aether.

Do not be frightened by this prospect. At all times during your astral travels, you will be in complete control of your aetheric body. There is no danger in emitting this internal aether. Start slowly, letting the aether come from your chest link like a steady stream of smoke or steam. It should coalesce just above you into a cloud of vaguely human form. Let your awareness gradually shift with this emission, your consciousness expanding to include the space above your physical body.

Emit enough aether to make a cloud about the size of your body, even if it seems a bit vapory. Now rest in this mode for a minute or so, your consciousness split between your material body and the cloud of aether above it.

Now stare into the cloud of aether and look at the face you've formed in it. Take some time to make sure the face remains as close as possible to your own, a steady vision with all the features there. The eyes are the same; the facial structure, the lips, nose, and hair are all the same. This is an important step, so take your time. There is no hurry.

Once your visualization is strong, hold it in your mind and feel your consciousness filling the cloud. The visualization of your face, and the eyes in particular, anchors your shifting consciousness as it moves from the space within your material body to the space just above it. Blink when you need to, keeping the face right above yours with those eyes blinking right back. Once you've brought your consciousness completely up to the floating space, blink again and realize that the face you see is no longer the face of your astral counterpart, that floating double made of so much of the stuff that is, essentially, you. No, the face you see is that of your material body, and you are looking down at it from above. Your consciousness is now floating freely above your physical form.

Your initial movement in your astral body shouldn't be too difficult if you take it slowly. Float higher into the room until your astral body is about five or six feet above you. Continue to focus on your face below so you don't get disoriented. Once you're high enough, lower your astral feet to the floor so that your astral body is standing upright. When this is done, take a deep breath or two and look around the room. What do you see? Is everything as you remember it?

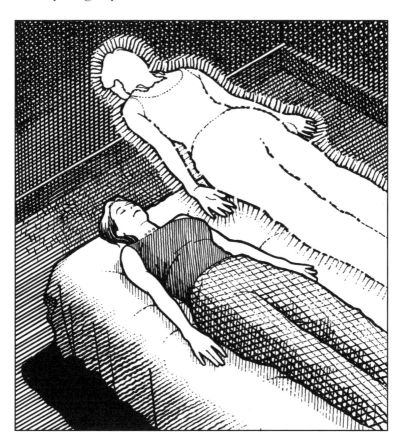

You will find that walking isn't really necessary while your consciousness is in this form. Simply think of where you want to move to, and you go gliding along, your feet just above the floor. Try it. Spend some time moving about the room or even the house in your astral form. Don't leave the house during this trip, though—the exercise following this one will guide you through your first "outdoor" astral trip.

Although it's unlikely, you may run into one or more spirits, elementals, or other aetheric beings on your initial journey. Do not be alarmed. Nearly all these beings are harmless, and most won't even notice you as they go about their otherworldly business. If you are ever frightened by them and do not wish to remain in their company, simply leave the area. If you feel safer nearer your physical body, move there.

When you're ready, begin to reintegrate your personal aether. Do this gradually, as a quick reconnection of your two selves can cause an unpleasant mental shock. Successful reintegration can be done by merely reversing the process by which you projected in the first place. Float your astral body above your prone material world form, ideally no more than twelve inches away. Align your astral face with your material counterpart, and focus on your breathing. Allow yourself to remember what everyday physicality is like, the way your material body feels. Let this feeling grow slowly in you, a gradual realization throughout your entire body as you shift your consciousness back to its earthly state.

Now close your eyes, breathe deeply, hold the breath, and as you exhale, open your eyes to see the ceiling of the room. You are back in your physical body. Gradually bring your vibration back to the material world. There's no need to rush. Relax and breathe for a minute or so in the material vibration. It is no doubt quite exhilarating.

You've just made your first astral journey away from your physical body. Way to go!

ASCENSION

This is a very exciting time in your aetheric development. You've just completed your first astral trip, and, although it was very brief, it was astoundingly important. This section will instruct you in your first astral excursion of any considerable length. You're well prepared for this trip, because it will take you on the same route you've been traveling on your walks around the neighborhood. This time, however, you will take your walk using your astral body.

Exercise 21: Your Astral Neighborhood

This exercise is best performed on a day when you've gone on your neighborhood walk, followed by a session of the aetheric dozen. Like the previous exercise, this one should be done lying down with the soles of your feet touching the wall. Go through the procedure of forming the astral body, floating it just above your prone form.

Once your consciousness has been transferred to this suspended body and you feel relaxed in it, bring your feet to the floor and look around the room. You have been outside your body at least once before. Do you notice that anything has changed from before? Look at your material form, breathing in unison with you. It will be fine while you are away. If you are ever in danger, your astral and material bodies will rejoin in an instant. Do not be afraid.

Now move from this room to the door of your house. Can you see the door plainly? Reach out and open it. "Walk" through and close the door behind you. Pause here. Remember to breathe.

Float several feet away from the door and look around. Take in the view—what do you see? Breathe deeply and savor the air. The air out here is different than that in your house. Give yourself a few seconds to get accustomed to this scene, and then begin your trip around the block.

Move at a normal pace along your path, if not a little slower than usual. There is a lot to see, a lot to hear. What do you notice? Does the sky seem familiar? Look at the buildings and the ground around you. Are there trees? Are there people? Keep moving but retain an active awareness of what's happening around you.

Continue your route to its farthest point, if you can, and then turn around and head for home. Aside from the floating, gliding attitude your body takes on during astral flight, remember to move as you normally would, using your hands to open and close the door when you return. Return to your practice space. You'll reintegrate your personal aether into your material body just as you did before, floating above and staring face-to-face into your own eyes. Keep breathing. Close your eyes and visualize your body growing more solid, more heavy, more anchored in the material world.

When you are back in your physical form—and when you are ready—open your eyes. It's natural to feel a bit disoriented after an astral projection session. Allow yourself time to regain your bearings once you've come back to the material vibration. Lie still and think about your trip. If you've maintained a slow, steady reduction in vibration on the way back down to the material world, you shouldn't have any adverse reaction to your projection. Take things slowly. You might even feel invigorated and excited once you're back. After all, you've just done something amazing!

Going Higher

If you've closely followed the directions given so far in this lesson, all your astral travels to this point have covered the same ground you've tread during your normal, material-world walks around your house and the neighborhood in which you live. No doubt you're hungering for something a little more spectacular in your astral projections. Perhaps you're thinking about flight to higher and more inaccessible places.

Even though humans are earthbound creatures by nature, we've all dreamed (while awake or asleep) of flying high above the earth at one time or another, hoping perhaps to escape from some dreary reality below or just to feel the thrill of unencumbered movement among the clouds.

This being the case, the barrier the aspiring mentalist has to surmount to achieve true astral flight (that is to say, astral flight unlimited by gravity) isn't the imagining of the act of flight—it's the visualization. As you know from your work so far, the imagination is the starting point for all mentalism, but before any imagined idea can have any validity in the material or astral world, it must be visualized with a great deal of concentration.

Everyday experiences can help you visualize astral flight. Within reason, you should have a material-world experience as close as possible to your astral flight.

I say "within reason" because I don't want to encourage you to put your physical body in danger as part of your aetheric studies. In fact, one of the greatest advantages of mentalism is that the aspirant can use his or her mind to do things that are impossible for the body to achieve.

So please don't go out and jump off a cliff in search of the feeling of flight necessary for this exercise. The aether in the astral world behaves like water at times, so if you are to excel at astral flight, it's good to have a working knowledge of how your body moves underwater. Swim often, taking careful note of how the water feels around your body. Scuba diving is also recommended, as the prolonged dives beneath the surface will accustom you to floating movement in another world.

Equally important to the sense of flight is a visual picture of what the earth looks like from above. Do you ever travel by plane? The next time you do, pay special attention to the ground below you. How does it look? Can you see your house from the air? Study maps of your hometown, paying close attention to your neighborhood. Then go outside and compare what you see on the maps to the actual houses and geographical features there. Stand on your roof and look around. How does your neighborhood look from up here? When you're ready, you should try to visit the skies above your town on the aetheric plane.

Psychic Residue

When you move on the aetheric plane, you leave a trail behind you, a psychic residue that is similar to the signs and scents left by an animal moving through the forest. This residual trail is made up of internal aether that breaks away from your aetheric body as you take in new experiences and sensations. In the material world as well as in the aetheric one, this trail also accounts in part for our ability to remember places we've been and things we've done. The trail is nearly imperceptible to beginning mentalists, who will see aetheric bodies as glowing forms that seem to be trailed by a blurred afterimage only a few inches in length. Experienced mentalists see the psychic residue clearly and can use it in tracking other aetheric beings or in determining what type of intelligences have come through an area in the astral world. It is this psychic residue trail that your astral body follows to get back to your material body. Even though it's best to retrace your steps back to your material body when finishing an astral trip, your consciousness and all your faculties are able to snap back instantly, if need be, by following the psychic residue trail.

AETHERIC HOUSEKEEPING

At times you may find it useful to clear out a roomlike space on the aetheric plane for use as a mental workshop. Perhaps you are plagued by distracting thoughts and need to focus your attention on a particular thing. Maybe you are unable to practice in your normal quiet space and need to find stillness in the midst of boisterous surroundings.

Recall the sugar exercise from earlier in this lesson. In it, you watched as a sugar cube dissolved slowly into the surrounding water. With proper visualization, you can mentally dissolve objects on the aetheric plane, temporarily obliterating their influence on you. This technique—like all others you are learning—is limited only by your imagination.

Exercise 22: Dissolution of Everyday Objects

Start out with this simple exercise. Clear your practice space of all objects save a chair, a book, a glass of water, and a pair of shoes. Sit in the chair, facing the objects, and enter a meditation in the lower astral frequency. Visualize the room, its walls defining the boundaries of the space that will become your aetheric workshop. Visualize the book, the glass of water, and the pair of shoes in the room, and also yourself in the chair. Think about the book; focus your attention on it. The book represents an object or thought standing in the way of your concentration. It must be removed from the space before you can continue. Look closely at the book (you can do this with your eyes open or closed, whichever feels more comfortable to you), so closely that you can see the texture of the cover. All surfaces have a texture, even if at first glance they appear smooth. Look at the texture of the cover of the book, and as you do, imagine an eddy of aether washing away at it. Bits flake off, float away from the cover, and dissolve into nothingness. Keep concentrating on the book. Once the cover is broken away and gone, let the pages come loose. See them float above the book and break apart rapidly, joining the eternal flow of the aether. Keep up this thought until the whole of the book has been dissolved. If you like, visualize a sharp spike of aether working away at the book, just like your pencil did to the sugar cube in the earlier exercise.

You might well wonder, is the book now destroyed? No, it is not—not in the slightest way. What you did was dissipate the thought of the book, the image of the book in your mind. If you look again, you may see the book back where it was, as solid as ever. Try not to let this happen as you move your attention to the glass of water and then to the shoes, dissipating each in the same way, as if they were made of sugar and submerged in a turbulent pool.

What difficulties do you notice as you dissolve these other objects? Does the glass shatter, or does it flake away like the book? Does the water in the glass steam as it disappears, or does it drain into nothingness, as if someone were drinking it with an invisible straw? Do you picture the laces of the shoe untying before they dissolve, the elements of the shoe coming apart as if it were being disassembled by hand, or does the shoe break up as if it were made of a single substance—as you and I know it truly is?

Once you've dissolved all three objects, rest a bit in your meditation and enjoy the room in its new uncluttered state. Does it take much effort to keep the objects invisible? Do they keep slipping back into view? Maintain the room's blank state for at least five minutes before allowing the objects to come back in. When you do, there is no need to rebuild them in the aether. You'll no doubt find that the objects reappear with little effort on your part. It's just a matter of noticing them again.

The paradox behind this exercise is that in the aether, thought is reality. The things you actively try not to think about are the very things that will crop up in front of you. It's vital that you learn to clear your mind of thought, making your self as blank as the room you've just cleared. This can only be done through regular meditation on the subject.

You may find it easy to dissolve things like books and glasses of water—all it may take is to close your eyes to forget about their presence. Out of sight, out of mind, after all. But what if you need to clear unwanted sounds from a room? What about smells? You must form techniques that help you clear these intruding sensations from your attention. Practice sitting in a crowded cafe, focusing on one conversation for a while and on another later. Then let the overall warble of voices merge, and, closing your eyes and your mental ears, dissolve the cacophony into nothing. Memorize scents, including the smell of nothing at all, and bring them back as needed. With practice this will become easier.

THE DWELLER ON THE THRESHOLD

The Lestrygonians and the Cyclops,
the fierce Poseidon you will never encounter,
if you do not carry them within your soul,
if your soul does not set them up before you.

—CONSTANTINE P. CAVAFY, *Ithaca*

Being human, each of us carries within ourselves a tremendous amount of psychic baggage. Most often the result of experiences gained in childhood, this mental burden weighs us down and hinders our capacity for mastery over aether. In order to move ahead in your studies of mentalism, it's necessary to take stock of your own burden and free yourself from its weight.

As it invariably does, the aether gives aspirants a very concrete representation of this psychic burden. It is called the Dweller on the Threshold, and you will meet it in the astral world early in your travels.

The Dweller's appearance is unique to everyone. One person's Dweller might appear as a great beast crouched in the middle of a road. To another person, the Dweller is a wall of fog or an endless field that cannot be crossed. No matter its appearance, in each case the Dweller's purpose is the same: to stop your aetheric advancement dead in its tracks.

It seems unfair, doesn't it? Here you are on the verge of great achievement on the aetheric plane, and this creature, this monstrosity, now stands in your way. Why?

That, dear aspirant, is a question that only you can answer. For just as the Dweller looks different to each and every one of us, so is the Dweller different. It is made up of all your past failings, your fears, your insecurities. Everything that's ever stopped you from fulfilling your desires and living out your dreams is bound up in the flesh of this unsettling creature, be it bottomless sea or stony serpent in appearance.

Facing the Dweller is not as awful a fate as you might think. In a way, the Dweller is giving you an opportunity, forcing you to come to grips with everything that's ever held you back, to examine why it is that you limit your own capacity—which is phenomenal—by believing falsehoods about who you are or what you can achieve. By setting it all before you now, when you are at the brink of terrific personal development, the Dweller is actually doing you a great favor.

Exercise 23: Crossing the Threshold

The ancient Egyptians, among others, believed in a being similar to the Dweller, one who guards the crossing point between life and death. The role of the aetheric Dweller you'll encounter isn't much different, for when you meet it you are ending your first life—that of a mundane—and stepping fully into your new life as a mentalist.

Despite its outward appearance, which as you know by now could be anything, the Dweller is not a single entity but an amalgam of legion thought-form elementals, each one representing a particular aspect of your life that has stifled you or held you back. Just like the Dweller, these creatures can appear as something completely unrelated to their true nature, but when you see each one, you'll soon realize what it is. These elementals will appear to you separate from the Dweller, breaking off from the greater form one by one. Each one must be met and understood for what part it has played in your life. It must then be dissipated using the technique you learned earlier in this lesson.

When you dissolve the elemental, you are not momentarily wiping it from your memory or temporarily clearing it from the space in which you are standing, like you did with the glass of water or the book. No, you're doing something much more powerful. By dissolving each elemental at the Threshold, you are accepting its influence in your life and making it clear that you will no longer let it hold you back.

The work you are doing here is mental—it is for the good of your mind. This process will not remove bad habits or unpleasant thoughts from your life, but it will stop you from being mentally restricted by them.

Expect the process to be emotional, as it is will bring up old memories and experiences that may have been swept under the rug. This process is also slow—do not expect it to be easy or fast. Take as much time as you need. It may take more than one session with the Dweller to overcome all its aspects. This is okay—there is no need to push yourself too hard. Take your time at the Threshold, long enough to appreciate what it is you're doing for yourself. You will appreciate the time you took, because the experience is deeply personal and rewarding, and it will make you a more whole person.

Once you have reconciled with the Dweller, you can pass freely across the Threshold and into the next stage of your mental development and your life. You will not meet this being again.

In a sense, crossing the Threshold will be one of the greatest feats of mentalism you will ever perform, because you will be overcoming yourself, your past, and all the things that have ever limited you.

All is aether.

Mentalism is will over aether.

And in the end, nothing's really holding you back, is it?

GOING ON

This lesson has outlined a number of practical exercises for the aspiring mentalist to perform in the astral world. No doubt you can think of many others you would like to try. By all means, experiment!

Practice your astral flight and attempt feats as they come to mind. Astral travel is a dynamic, fantastic experience. Try to get the most from it. Use the skills you've learned in your practice here to do things you wouldn't normally try with your material body, to go places that are physically impossible for you to visit.

Try the psychism experiments you learned earlier in this book. You may find clairvoyance, telepathy, and telekinesis to be surprisingly different while projecting. Notice how your thoughts affect your surroundings, how even your daydreams alter the environment in a subtle way.

Keep an eye out for other aetherics in the astral world. Most of them are benign, many not even paying much attention to you. You are all like fish swimming in a vast ocean, each inhabitant going about its own business. All the same, remain aware that there are aetheric beings out there that wish harm on others. The aether is a "transparent" substance in that a being's motive or purpose is often clear when you encounter it, but powerful aetherics can throw up a mental smoke screen that masks their true intentions. Be careful.

Above all, enjoy your new knowledge and work to use the aether in a meaningful way. Keep practicing the aetheric dozen, and meditate on what the aether means to you.

DE MORTUIS NIHIL NISI BONUM

LESSON FIVE.
THE SPIRIT WORLD

The Living and the Dead—Centuries of Spiritism—Spiritism Today—Questions from Readers—Aether and the Afterlife—Where Do We Go When We Die?—A Word for Believers—Another for Nonbelievers—The Nature of Spirits—Human Spirits—Animal Spirits—Phantoms—Mediums among Us—The New New World—Strengthening Attention—The Power of Phantoms—A Phantom Companion—Reaching Out—Sensing Spirits—Spiritism in Everyday Life—Spirits Surround Us—Even You

"There is no death, there are no dead."
—INSCRIPTION ON THE MEMORIAL STONE OUTSIDE
THE FOX FAMILY COTTAGE, HYDESVILLE, NEW YORK

DO YOU KNOW SOMEONE WHO HAS DIED? Would you like to see their face again or speak to them once more, even if it is just to tell them you love them? Do you ever wonder if plants can think or if they have souls? What does it mean when some of your possessions mean more to you than some of your friends? The practice of spiritism—a specialization of mentalism—allows you to look for answers to these questions. By using your basic understanding of the aether, you now have a chance to explore the spirit world and meet its inhabitants, be they the aetheric doubles of humans, plants, animals, or even seemingly inanimate objects.

During life, the aetheric body can be used for many things. It is useful for performing psychisms, such as the clairvoyance and telekinesis exercises you've tried. Astral projection is a practice you learned in the previous lesson, and by now you've no doubt found a number of advantages to knowing this skill. One use you may wish to develop further is the ability to hold congress with other aetheric doubles.

The spirit world is a bustling, exciting place. By practicing the spiritism exercises presented in this lesson, you'll gain access to this fascinating realm, a place few people see during earthly life.

THE LIVING AND THE DEAD

Centuries of Spiritism

Spirits have appeared in mankind's stories since the dawn of time. The earliest mention of a spirit in a written story occurs in the *Epic of Gilgamesh,* a Babylonian tale dated around 2000 BCE. Belief in the souls of the dead returning to the world of the living goes back much further, though. Excavated remains from prehistoric gravesites have shown that some of our ancestors were buried with hands and feet bound together or weighted down with stones, leading archeologists to believe that early man meant to hinder the return of the spirit. Other cultures have similar traditions, which they carry out even today.

The modern spiritism movement traces its roots back to the Swedish philosopher Emanuel Swedenborg, a mentalist and author who visited the spirits of kings, popes, and saints, writing of his experiences and founding a spiritualist church. Swedenborg's work greatly influenced later spirit world investigators, including William Blake.

Authorship makes us all immortal, in a way, but Swedenborg was apparently not content with mere indirect influence on future generations of mentalists. Nearly eighty years after his death, Swedenborg's spirit, along with the ghost of second-century Greek thinker Claudius Galen, appeared to the American shoemaker Andrew Jackson Davis. The ensuing conversation between the three changed Davis's life, and within two years he had produced the spiritist manifesto *The Principles of Nature, Her Divine Revelations, and a Voice to Mankind,* in which he predicted that proof of the spirit world would manifest in "a living demonstration."

After publication of *The Principles,* Davis waited for such a phenomenon to occur, and on March 31, 1848, he entered the following passage in his notebook: "About daylight this morning a warm breathing passed over my face and I heard a voice, tender and strong, saying: 'Brother, the good work has begun— behold a living demonstration is born.'"

That very same day, two young girls in Hydesville, New York, began their soon-to-be famous communications with the spirit world. Seven-year-old Kate Fox and her ten-year-old sister Margaret came into contact with the ghost of a murdered peddler living in their family's cottage. They found the spirit could answer questions posed to it by making sharp rapping sounds (one for yes, two for no) that could not otherwise be accounted for.

The congruence of Davis's notebook entry and the beginning of the Fox sisters' mediumship ushered in an era of intense interest in spiritism that consumed American and European society. Kate and Margaret Fox toured both continents, giving presentations of their remarkable abilities. London's Ghost Club and the British Society for Psychical Research were founded to further investigate the spirit world. Séances became regular happenings at bourgeois and upper-class homes, and general interest in spirits reached a level not seen before or since.

Spiritism Today

The fervor associated with the spiritism craze of the late nineteenth century has died down, but people today have some of the same experiences as the mediums of yesteryear. Ouija boards and books on the subject of spirits continue to sell well. Mediums advertise in your local newspaper, and television shows feature evangelistic spiritists who promise to bring viewers in touch with the spirits of their loved ones.

Ghosts do not start or stop appearing just because they are popular. They couldn't care less about fads, ads, or television programs. No, spirits have their own reasons, their own agendas. In this lesson we will examine the various beings waiting to communicate with us from beyond the veil of death and how we can seek them out ourselves.

Questions from Readers

Before we begin our examination of the different types of aetheric doubles that make up the spirit world, allow me to answer a few common questions about the subject.

What do spirits look like?

Popular culture, such as that presented to us by books and films, paints a somewhat limited picture of the average spirit. It is often pictured as a semitransparent figure, perhaps dressed in flowing robes or a sheet, emitting a low moaning sound. This is not always how a spirit appears to us. As you'll find, spirits are seldom as "ghostly" as we might imagine them to be. Quite often, in fact, spirits look exceedingly solid and "real," and you may not realize you have been visited by one until it does something out of the ordinary, such as walk through a wall or appear or disappear abruptly—"into thin air," you might say—although the spirit is merely flitting its visible form in and out of the material world vibration.

Why do spirits return to the material world?

While some spirits' motives will never be discerned, people fortunate enough to be visited by a spirit sometimes learn why it has returned. Some spirits wish to communicate with a loved one or a person they didn't have a chance to bid farewell before leaving this world. Others come to issue a warning or to give information that would never be discovered otherwise. Rare is the spirit who seeks revenge, but they do exist. More often a spirit comes to see that justice is done, that a culprit is found out or that the innocent are protected.

How is it that spirits walk through walls?

This is an interesting question, as it would appear that some spirits have a mastery over solid objects such as walls and doors and may pass through them with ease. If you chance to see a spirit pass through a solid wall, for example, pay close attention to the spirit's other movements and mannerisms—you may be surprised at what you notice. It is likely that the spirit can pass through the wall not because it has power over the corporeality of the wall, but because the spirit is very much removed from the reality in which the wall exists. Perhaps the spirit lived in human form on earth in a time before the wall was constructed, or perhaps the spirit has such a great need to get from one place to another that it will not let material-world impediments get in its way.

One way we can compare this phenomenon with things that go on in our own lives is to think about what happens when we are "lost in thought." Have you ever been so deep in your own head as you walk through your house or down the street that you run right into some obstruction, such as a wall or post? Some would say that we hit these barriers because we are not paying attention. In truth, we *are* paying attention, just not to the material world around us but to an interior world of our own construction.

The difference between the spirit's passing through the wall and our colliding with it lies in the degree to which the spirit is immersed in the interior world of the aetheric plane. When humans are lost in their own thoughts, they are still a part of the physical world. Spirits do not have such a strong connection to earthly life and so are less affected by it.

Why is it that when spirits are present they are sometimes seen and sometimes unseen?

If only spirits would act in a consistent manner, then we could say so much more about their true nature! Alas, it is not to be. Spirits may appear to be of solid form or may seem ghostly, and in some cases they will not be visible at all. This phenomenon is partly explained by the aforementioned flickering of the spirit between the astral and material-world vibrations.

Remember, too, that in the aether our perception of reality is continually influenced by the notions and needs of other aetheric beings in the vicinity. When our own mental picture of life is weaker than that of another aetheric's, our reality and perception can be overruled to accommodate their own. When spirits make themselves known to us, it is often because their presence in the aether is so strong that their form crosses the normal boundaries of perception.

AETHER AND THE AFTERLIFE

When we talk of spirits, we generally think of them as beings different than ourselves, but the truth, as you will learn, is otherwise. Your aetheric studies thus far have taught you the basics of aether and the aetheric plane, as well as some fundamental exercises with which to strengthen your control over this universal substance. Most recently, you learned about astral projection, the practice of moving the consciousness (also known as your internal aether) away from the physical body and traveling free of all ties to the material world. Many names were assigned to the vessel you traveled in—the astral body, the mind, and the self, among others. Now we will make two very important additions to that list, for your internal aether also goes by the names of *spirit* and *soul*.

The truth is that you are also a spirit, different in no way from the ghosts of the realm of the dead except that you inhabit a fleshy form in the material world, one that you will shed upon physical death as you rejoin your brethren in the eternal aether. The experience we know as physical life is merely a transition between our soul's eternal existence before and after this earthly interlude.

Spirits have throughout history perplexed and frightened most people, and they probably always will. As representatives of the world of the dead, spirits are certainly strange to us and can seem scary. But what do we have to be afraid of, really? If indeed the spirits of the dead are merely the disembodied doubles of those once living, then these spirits are probably not far removed in temperament from their former selves, and meeting one of them might be no more dangerous than meeting any other new person.

Among your meetings in the aether you might find a spirit still clinging to memories of earthly life (a being known as a revenant), or you may encounter a soul at eternal rest upon whom you can call for knowledge of another time or place. Meetings with these spirits seem less alien and bizarre once you realize how close you yourself are to them (especially when you are traveling in your aetheric form, removed from your physical body), although to call the encounters more "human" would be missing the point.

All this is simple to state but may be difficult to believe. I don't ask you to take my word on it. Instead, do your own investigation using the aetheric skills you've already learned. With time and practice you will no doubt come to your own understanding of an eternal life existing before and after earthly life, if for no other reason than that this theory makes more sense than one stating that life begins and ends with the birth and death of our material bodies, given what we know about the power of the human consciousness and its potential for feats unexplained by everyday logic.

Your discoveries may serve as a balm to you when thinking of loved ones who have passed out of this life. They are not as far away as you think, and your studies of mentalism and the aether are bringing you closer to them every day.

Where Do We Go When We Die?

If you were brought up with any sort of religious or spiritual background, you've no doubt spent a lot of time thinking about the spirit or soul, an entity that survives death. Belief in the afterlife is nearly universal among adherents of the world's major religions, but nothing could be more diverse than the theories describing what happens to that soul after death. Here are notes on the beliefs of four major religions regarding the soul and the afterlife.

Hinduism: Hindu belief dictates the existence of an individual soul known as the Atman, or deep self. The Atman is truly immortal in that it is a fragment separated from the greater godhead of Brahma, the universal soul from which all life is formed. Through a succession of material incarnations, the Atman strives to reunite with Brahma in the afterlife by doing good deeds while on earth.

Serving the function of a cosmic scorecard, the natural law of karma keeps track of an individual's deeds, rewarding good behavior and punishing evil acts. It is necessary for the soul to be reincarnated on earth in order to "reap the karma" on the way to eventual enlightenment and reintegration with the godhead.

Ancient Hindus held that for individual spirits this reintegration would feel like being a drop of water falling into the sea, the individual's personality obliterated as it merged with the oversoul and yielded to a state of eternal bliss. This belief was challenged by adherents of devotionalism, who claimed that in the afterlife the soul would retain individuality and would enjoy a never-ending blissful existence worshiping the godhead.

Hindus believe in a number of places of spiritual punishment where the souls of evil people meet tortures according to their misdeeds. Eventually, though, even these souls are reincarnated to live out another life on earth.

Judaism: The afterlife is less of a concern than the present life to followers of Judaism, but the history of this faith reveals an interesting variety of beliefs about the fate of the human soul. Early Jewish belief in the afterlife mirrored that of the Mesopotamians and Greeks, speaking of a shadowy existence in a dull netherworld known as Sheol. They thus strove to live life to the fullest while on earth. God was believed to have a covenant with man, giving rewards and punishments during life, not after death.

As the centuries passed, it became clear that not all people were meeting with divine justice in this life, and among some of the mystics a reincarnation theory arose, granting second chances on earth for individuals who had committed the most horrendous sins.

While some Jews share a belief in a heaven or hell similar to that of the Christians, there are a number of opinions among Orthodox, Secular, and Reform Jews as to the nature of the soul and its fate after bodily death.

Christianity: Christianity developed a keen interest in the afterlife almost immediately upon the faith's inception. The bodily resurrection of Christ was the model for the Christian belief in mass bodily resurrection for all of mankind on the Day of Judgment, the pious going to the blissful heaven and the wicked to the torturous hell.

Other cultures have had a marked influence on Christian beliefs relating to the afterlife and the soul. Early Christians borrowed their belief in an apocalyptic world from their Jewish contemporaries. The idea of the immortality of the soul came from the Hellenistic beliefs of the Romans and Gnostic Greeks.

After death, the human soul is assigned to one of three possible places—heaven, hell, or purgatory, an intermediary between the extremes of joy and agony where the soul may be cleansed before gaining admission into heaven. The Protestant sect of the sixteenth century rejected the notion of purgatory, claiming that salvation and entrance to paradise is granted by the grace of God.

Islam: Another faith with strong beliefs in the eternal soul and rewards and punishments in the afterlife is the Muslim system, or Islam. After bodily death, the soul (known as nafs) is separated from the physical body and travels to Barzakh, a place where it gains knowledge of its true nature. The soul stays in this dreamlike place until the Day of Judgment, at which time it is assigned to hell or heaven based on its deeds during earthly life.

The Muslim paradise promises all manner of pleasure to the believers. This heaven is arranged in a spherical, many-layered manner, surrounding God, and the Islamic hell borders this paradise's outermost layer. Assignment to hell can be temporary, the soul gaining admission to heaven after its earthly sins have been burned away.

Islamic opinions vary on the exact relationship of the soul and the material body after death. Sunni Muslims hold that both the soul and the physical body die at the moment of earthly death. A second death comes after a trial overseen by a godlike judge and two angels. Upon this second death, the soul is obliterated until its reunion with the physical body on Judgment Day. Shiite Muslims believe in the commencement of rewards and punishments for the soul upon bodily death. The soul rejoins the physical body upon the Day of Judgment, and its stay in heaven or hell continues for eternity.

A Word for Believers

Many aspiring mentalists are believers in one religious faith or another, and they often wonder if the aether runs counter to their faith. Some ask how it is possible to believe in God and aether at the same time. You need not reject God or mentalism just because your religion teaches nothing of the aether. For many people, God is the supreme embodiment of aether and the originator of the aetheric plane. It is not sacrilegious to think that there is a structure and system underlying all of creation.

Another for Nonbelievers

It can be troubling to some people, looking at all the various theories of the afterlife and wondering which one of them, if any, reflects the actual journey of the soul upon bodily death. Even stranger than any of the above theories is the actual truth: that they are all true.

Just as an individual's faith and concentrated belief can change the aether in the material world, so centuries of strong belief by millions of religious adherents have sustained the various heavens, hells, and systems of rebirth. It is important, therefore, not to discount another person's spiritual beliefs, and it is equally important to know where your own faith lies.

THE NATURE OF SPIRITS

Because the aether composes absolutely everything, the aetheric plane contains a counterpart for every man, woman, and child, every animal and plant, and every object in existence. Knowledge of these doubles is important, because as you proceed in your studies of mentalism, you will encounter them all.

The doubles of living beings dwell in the aether both during life and after the death or destruction of their physical forms. During life, they exist in an aetheric location comparable to their place in the material world. After death the doubles are known as spirits, and they may no longer be under any obligation to stay near their former earthly body. The doubles of inanimate objects mirror the state of their material counterparts and remain in a space in the aether corresponding to the matter and mass of their earthly forms. Mentalists have never been able to pinpoint in the aether the locations of realms such as the Christian hell or heaven, and some believe that these places are not actual locations at all, but rather states of being incomprehensible to the living.

The spirits remaining in the astral vibration after death make up the segment of the spirit world most accessible to us as mentalists. Their reasons for pausing in the astral world are various, as will be explained in the remainder of this section. With few exceptions, rapport with these aetheric beings is no more or less difficult than conversation with new people you might meet in the material world.

Human Spirits

There are four classes of human spirits you can expect to encounter in the astral world, three of them the spirits of the dead and one—the lost soul— the disembodied spirit of someone yet living.

Departed Spirits: As you learned in the previous essay, human souls undergo different afterlife experiences after death. Some are immediately transported to places of eternal torture or reward, others are put in a sort of cosmic waiting room where they remain until an apocalyptic day of reckoning occurs. Still other souls are seemingly obliterated, reduced to a non-sensory existence while they, too, wait for judgment. Finally, some souls are part of a cycle of reincarnation, inhabiting the afterworld for a time between their rounds on earth.

It may surprise you to know that some of these souls wish to communicate with those still living an earthly life. Whether they manifest themselves to us in the material world or while we project our consciousnesses into the aether, departed spirits often have a message they want us to hear. Sometimes spirits are known to appear at the moment of their earthly death, yet miles from their physical bodies. This type of spirit is called a crisis apparition, and it shows itself to loved ones in an attempt to make its goodbyes to the material world.

Other times the spirits of the departed return to deliver a message of love or comfort to friends and relatives distraught over their death. These visits are usually single, solitary events, but they occasionally occur again and again over time.

Spirits are sometimes sought out by surviving family members or others who wish to speak with the departed. This is the purpose of the séance.

Other departed spirits have no connection at all to the living people who see them. If the visit is merely to impart information useful to those of us still on earth, the ghost can rightly be classified as a departed spirit. If, however, the spirit needs something from us in response to its appearing, that spirit may be a revenant.

Revenants: These are the aetheric bodies of people who, even though dead, have unfinished business in the land of the living. They remain near the place they occupied during life, floating between the lower astral and the material-aetheric vibrational frequencies. They are often seen performing tasks indicative of their time on earth. Revenants are popular in literature, and if the folktales of countless cultures are to be any guide, these spirits need the intervention of a living being to settle their cosmic accounts here on earth.

Revenants are not always powered by greed or memories of material life. Other forces can keep them bound to earth. Some people die and cannot fully move on to the afterlife because of a strong belief that it does not exist or that it is remarkably different from what they are experiencing in the aether. Others spend their time as revenants because they don't realize they are dead—they go on with their day-to-day activities as if nothing has changed save a noticeable disregard from their colleagues. Of those who understand their earthly demise, a sense of purpose regarding their death takes hold of some spirits, and they feel they must learn more about its cause or warn others still living about whatever was their undoing. Finally, some spirits are kept earthbound by mourners whose constant thoughts about the deceased hold the aetheric body near, in much the same way thought-form elementals are created and sustained.

In order for a revenant to be released from its bondage to the material world, its questions or conflicts regarding life and death must be laid to rest by someone still living. Because mentalists are especially skilled at communication with spirits, this task is often up to them.

Wraiths: When a soul has unfinished matters on earth and needs human intervention to come to rest, it is a revenant. When a soul seeks out this intervention through destructive deeds, it is a wraith.

Wraiths are perhaps the most dangerous and treacherous aetheric beings you will encounter in your travels on the astral plane. They are usually invisible, even when vibrating on the same frequency as other aetherics around them, but they can be detected by the tight, suffocating air that surrounds them. Some theories hold that this phenomenon is a natural extension of the wraith's aetheric form, others state that the tightness is the result of a sense of repulsion that the surrounding aether feels toward this being, a sort of communal thought-form elemental of dread formed by the aether itself.

Whatever the case, wraiths hold unbelievable power over the aether. The hate and jealousy seething throughout their form gives them great levels of telekinesis, telepathy, and clairvoyance but relatively little control over the power.

Wraiths are very scattered aetherically, their thoughts and personality so random in life that in death their aetheric body is thin, spread out, and amorphous, exercising a mild influence over a large area around their body's resting place, sometimes through vapors (see this book's aetheric bestiary for a description of vapors). This wispy aether accounts in part for the chills you may get when visiting a graveyard or the site of a violent death.

Wraiths strengthen their insubstantial forms by draining the internal aether of any hapless humans they meet on the astral plane. The wraith will seek control over one or more of the projected body's aetheric links, usually the chest or forehead link, in an attempt to paralyze the being. Once this is done, the wraith begins sapping the body's aether, adding it to its own and bringing more corporeality to its form. The aether available in a projected body is not usually sufficient to complete this transformation, so all too soon the wraith sends mental feelers along the trail of psychic residue leading back to the material body. Once these feelers find their way to the physical body, they open a conduit through which the remaining internal aether of the victim can flow. A person thus attacked by a wraith is in grave danger and will likely enter a coma or die if some intervening measure is not taken.

To protect against aether drain by a wraith, mentalists are advised to travel in pairs when visiting dangerous areas on the astral plane. Because the wraith must invest a large amount of concentration on the initial seizing of the aetheric link, a nearby partner can be a lifesaver, as he or she can snap back to the material vibration and arouse the victim's physical body before the attack is complete.

Recovery from a wraith attack is for the most part swift. What personal aether is lost in the attack is replaced by aether from food, water, stimulating conversation or activity, or simply through rest and meditation in the material world. It's natural to be frightened of astral projection after going through such an experience, but you must remember that just by surviving such an attack you will eventually gain back everything that was lost.

Lost Souls: Occasionally a person's aetheric body will separate from its material counterpart involuntarily, in part or in whole, leaving the person incapacitated. The escaped aetheric body is known as a lost soul.

There are several circumstances under which a split like this may occur. Most revolve around what has become known as the near-death experience. People who undergo a sudden physical shock sometimes report that they experience a separation of the consciousness or self (what you and I refer to as the aetheric body) from their gross material form. The aetheric body floats upward and looks down upon its material-world counterpart. It is rare for these accounts to include any anxiety or negative emotion from the victim, as panic-inducing as such a situation would seem. Almost invariably, the disembodied spirit feels an overwhelming sense of peace and may regard those below itself on earth quizzically, wondering what the great rush is to shorten the serenity it has found in the aether.

From here the experience either ends abruptly with the rousing of the incapacitated fleshy body or continues with a brief astral voyage on the part of the lost soul. The spirit travels through the aether to a portal between this world and the afterlife, and it must make a choice.

Understandably, most of the accounts we have from this voyage are from those who chose to come back to this world despite the peacefulness they found in the aether. But what of those who fall into long periods of unconsciousness, those who remain living but spend day after day in a coma or otherwise vegetative state? Their personality has departed and yet they live. What becomes of their aetheric bodies?

While there are exceptions, based on our investigations it is safe to assume that their sublime selves travel in the astral world as lost souls. They have chosen the serenity of the aether, and—while they are not physically dead—their earthly bodies are inert and useless.

Some souls wander the aether aimlessly, appearing as glowing, ghostlike apparitions to those who encounter them in the astral world. They are lost in their own thoughts, mildly confused but peaceful enough in their wanderings that without intervention by another being (such as a mentalist projecting into the aether), nothing will alarm them or suggest that they should return to their material bodies and lives.

Here let us pause for a moment to address an important point that many aspiring mediums raise regarding the ways in which the various classes of human spirits differ in appearance. Students ask me questions such as, "How can I tell a revenant from a wraith?" and "What do lost souls look like?" This is what I tell them:

These are good questions and ones that are not easily answered. The distinction between a revenant and a wraith is one of the most important ones you can make, as the price of failure can be terrible. For the most part, wraiths emit a chilling force through the aether that should alert even the most casual astral traveler to their presence. If seen, a wraith will often appear less substantial than other spirits you've encountered, usually to the point of taking on a vaporous quality.

Be aware, though, that wraiths are not the only members of the spirit world that may wish you harm. Revenants are rightfully listless after long periods of solitude, and while they are not evil by intention, some of their actions and involvements with the living may seem extremely selfish. Be wary of this and avoid being taken advantage of by spirits, no matter what situation you find them in.

Lost souls are actually quite easy to spot. Wandering without any sense of where they are or where they are going, these spirits stumble through the aether like blindfolded men on a busy sidewalk. Because of their connection to a living body in the material world, these astral bodies glow a bit brighter than the surrounding aether. Although some unscrupulous aetherics have taken to impersonating lost souls for the purpose of tricking the mentalists who would help them, this sort of treachery is rare.

Animal Spirits

The spirits of animals are peculiar things indeed. They embody the traits of their material-world counterparts, but they have some mysterious qualities as well. The majority of animal spirits you encounter will be not so dissimilar from everyday animals you are used to seeing. These are not the only animal spirits wandering the aether, however.

Departed Animal Spirits: The aetheric doubles of animals live on after bodily death in the same manner as those of humans. Instead of heavens or hells or reincarnations, however, animal souls are assigned to a location in the aether of one of the other worlds, be it the elemental, astral, or elysian. Here the animals spend eternity, assisting other aetheric beings or just prowling and lurking in the wilds of aetheric space. Animal spirits in the elemental world take on the qualities of lesser salamanders, sylphs, undines, or gnomes, depending on their assignment (see the aetheric bestiary for more information on each of these elementals). Elysium provides safe haven for the spirits of animals, and they may find themselves the companions of one of the native creatures there.

Animal spirits in the astral world retain most of the functions and personality traits they held in the material world, and they may be called upon for aid or guidance when necessary. More often, though, the spirit of the animal will come at an unexpected, though fortuitous, time, intervening in a dangerous situation to prevent harm to beings yet living.

Sometimes, an animal spirit will appear to signal a death in the family. The spirit of a dog or cat will occasionally adopt a family for generations, making itself visible a day or so before the loss of one of the family members.

Archetypes: Greater animal spirits are called archetypes. These beings are composite spirits made up of a number of animal (and sometimes human) souls to create a powerful aetheric being. Archetypes are worshiped by aboriginal, animistic cultures around the world. Whole tribes and cults can spring up around the veneration of wolf or bear spirits, for example. Less common are archetypes made of two or more species of animal, and the cults based on them are quite rare. Examples of these monstrosities include the gryphon and the chimera.

Eternal Animals: While similar to archetypes, eternal animals are even more rare than their composite cousins. The phoenix and the dragon come to mind, along with all other creatures of myth with characteristics utterly distinct from any living animal. These beings are not usually found in the astral vibration, instead making their home in the lofty elysian world.

Phantoms

Two types of phantoms exist in the aether, the doubles of nonsentient objects and the doubles of plants.

Doubles of Nonsentient Objects: Everyday objects have their own doubles on the aetheric plane. In most cases, calling these entities spirits would be a stretch. However, some objects are imbued with enough meaning and significance on earth that their double develops a personality of its own. Think of your favorite possessions from childhood or family heirlooms passed from previous generations to your own. Practically speaking, these objects are no more than simple toys or trinkets, but years and years of attention have increased their significance to the point where you may see them as something more special. This is especially apparent when you look at these objects' aetheric doubles during your meditations. Ancient cultures believed in a material object's usefulness crossing the boundary between this world and the next, and they buried useful tools with their dead. While this practice has died out somewhat, phantoms are still very much useful to us in our aetheric studies.

Material objects can also carry qualities of the substances from which they were made, such as wood or petroleum, into the aetheric plane. All manufactured objects are made from something that was once alive, even if this "family tree" must be traced back a few generations to find a living ancestor. Thus the spirits of trees can sometimes be found in the houses constructed from them, and metallic jewelry can retain a trace of the elemental forces of the mine from which it was wrought.

Plant Doubles: Science has recently shown us that plants have a certain intelligence of their own. "Rudimentary" is the closest word we have in English to describe the nature of plantlife intelligence, but closer to the truth, it's better to say that plants have an extremely slow (by human standards) mental process. What's even more amazing is that this thinking process is one that is *shared* among all plants as a whole. Plants "talk" to each other through various chemical and aetheric exchanges. A redwood tree might lend its ancient wisdom to new saplings of other species budding elsewhere on the forest floor, for example.

Plantlife has a unique signature in the astral world. The space around the base of a tree will glow with a green energy that offsets the usual blue tinge of the astral world. Just as in the material world, each part of the plant has a different function in the aether. Roots draw elemental energy from the soil and water below, trunks act as beacons and antennae for communication within the matrix of plant intelligence, branches and leaves reach out for interactions with the rest of the aether and also transmit psychic messages that can be understood by other plants and, in some cases, by carefully attuned animals and humans.

Fruit is a powerful tool among plants, and, as with most things, its aetheric function is tied closely to the role it plays on earth. Through fruit (or spores, when dealing with fungi), plants maintain a nearly immortal status. Each fruit contains a concentrated mass of aether that holds the plant's entire history and the collective knowledge of the plant's ancestors. When the fruit is dropped to earth, it does one of three things: its seed grows into another plant of the same species; it is eaten by a human or animal, which then drops the fruit's seeds elsewhere; or it is absorbed into the soil around it. All of these functions occur in the aether as well. Think of the fruit as a letter, a message, or an autobiography of the plant from which it dropped. In the aether, dropped fruit may be used as such and read like a book by those tuned in to its relatively low aetheric frequency around the border of the material and elemental worlds.

The Biblical tale of Adam, Eve, and the Tree of Knowledge of Good and Evil provides a terrific example of how fruit can be used not only for physical sustenance but for mental development as well. Eat your fruit.

MEDIUMS AMONG US

You have learned much about spirits in your readings so far, but the written word can describe only so much, so your studies must extend beyond it and into the spirit world itself, where there is much to learn.

Mentalists who focus their aetheric studies on the spirit world are known as spiritists or, more commonly, mediums. The medium is a sort of specially tuned astral traveler, one who pays closer attention to the relationships among aetheric beings, particularly the spirits of the dead, although the medium regularly examines phantoms and the aetheric doubles of the living. The priests and spiritual advisors among so-called primitive peoples are good examples of mediums who deal with all manner of spirits.

What makes a medium? There are a few things that distinguish mediums from other mentalists. Mediums maintain a profound belief in the immortality of the aetheric body, faith that this aspect of living things survives the death of the physical body and lives on, either on the aetheric plane at one vibration or another or by coming back to earth for reincarnation in a new form. Some spiritists hold that our souls come back to inhabit human bodies exclusively; others believe that the aetheric double of a human can return as that of an animal or plant. Theories are as multifarious as those of the religions that inevitably spring up around such beliefs.

The medium makes regular attempts at contact and communication with the spirits of the dead. Reasons for this discourse are varied—curiosity of the unknown is a common factor among most spiritists, but other reasons exist. Some wish to communicate with the recently deceased, perhaps to put loved ones still living in contact with these souls. Some mediums volunteer with law enforcement agencies to help with homicide cases or otherwise lend their services to those without access to the aether. They sometimes investigate hauntings, which are not common but are underreported by the press. Another sort of medium acts as a type of Good Samaritan for souls in need, helping revenants settle their karmic debt and guiding lost souls back to their material bodies.

People who have seen spirits without any preparation or training are more apt to be successful as mediums. They are very likely already vibrating a bit high in the material-aetheric world to begin with and may find all mentalism practices—not just spiritism—to come a bit easier than their more "grounded" colleagues.

A medium is constantly aware of the dual nature of all things. For him or her, nothing on earth can be taken at face value—everything has an aetheric counterpart that must be considered.

The New New World

With the spirit world incorporating the phantoms of plants and inanimate objects among the already burgeoning population of human and animal spirits of the dead and doubles of the living, you'll find this realm an incredibly rich place for exploration. The closest parallel one could draw to explorations of the material world would be the voyages of James Cook, Christopher Columbus, and Ferdinand Magellan—or, to use a contemporary example, the investigations of the earth's oceans currently underway. In the case of the early explorers, the discoveries made aboard their ships and in the various lands they found altered the basic worldviews of their countrymen, as no doubt will our findings under the surface of the sea. But what can these forays into the unknown be called if not incomplete—naïve even—compared to the explorations you can now undertake in the aether, a place where one can communicate with every imaginable thing: the spirits of the dead, the plants and animals, even the air and the ocean itself?

Indeed, the initial question most new travelers in the spirit world face is not "Where should I go?" but "Where does one begin?" There can be so much activity packed into a small area in the aether that to go in unprepared is ill advised. Attention-strengthening exercises are a good way to prepare yourself for your interactions in the spirit world.

Exercise 24: Strengthening Attention

The next time you're in a crowded or cacophonous place in the material world—a mall or busy restaurant, for example—take some time to concentrate on individual sights and sounds around you. You may think this would come easily, especially the idea of training your eye on one particular thing at the expense of all others. Try it, and you may find it a greater challenge than you expected.

Focus your gaze on something simple—a potted plant in the mall, for example. Interesting looking people may walk by; loud sounds or strong smells may vie for your attention. You must not let them have it. Can you stare at the plant for ten whole minutes without breaking your gaze except to blink?

Listening to one conversation in the din and then refocusing your attention to a fainter conversation somewhere else can be a much more difficult task but interesting and rewarding enough to merit much practice. Perhaps it's possible to try it in the same busy place where you just looked at the plant. Anywhere there are lots of conversations going on is a good place to practice this exercise.

You may find that a certain person's voice will naturally make itself clear among all the others. Mentally latch on to this voice and listen closely. Close your eyes if it helps.

More important than the physical act of looking or listening is your concentration on the subject itself. It's one thing to stare at a plant for ten minutes or to keep track of the sound of two voices having a conversation. But how long can you look at the plant and think "plant" above all other thoughts or put yourself in its place? How long can you follow the conversation the strangers are having and actively think about it, drawing conclusions about the people talking or the subject they are discussing?

Developing this type of attention will bring you closer to the spirits or doubles you will soon observe in the aether. A strong attention serves us well in the material world as well as in the aether. Increased powers of attention help with reading, meditation, conversation, studying, and many other tasks you perform on a regular basis.

The Power of Phantoms

Phantoms—the aetheric doubles of inanimate objects—are the least understood of all the inhabitants of the spirit world. For the most part, phantoms are useful to mediums and astral travelers as sources of energy, repositories of aether of a quality related to the material object. Personal effects are often the most powerful transmitters of this type of energy, and it's easy to explain totems, fetishes, and charms using this model of aetheric thought. The objects from childhood that we keep into our adult lives are imbued with so much meaning to us that this naturally translates to a strong material and aetheric connection between the object and its owner.

In this way, a teddy bear helps us feel comforted and protected on earth, but in the aether it can be much more powerful. From its protective energy—which has been concentrated for decades, perhaps—you could use your visualization skills to construct an aetheric shield, a cocoon, or even a vessel to carry you safely from place to place. As usual, your only limits are the boundaries of your own imagination.

Exercise 25: A Phantom Companion

Choose an object you've owned since childhood and focus on it during your next meditation session. Concentrate on the associations it brings up in your mind, the emotions it makes you feel.

Try to remember specific events in your life when the object was near and think about how your associations with this thing are formed from those experiences. Spend at least half an hour thinking about this while you're in a material-world (nonastral) meditation and record your impressions afterward. List the emotions you felt during your meditation and write down a few experiences you've had with the object during your life.

Do this again a day or two later, with another childhood object of yours, writing down your impressions later. If your first object was something that brought to mind pleasant or happy feelings, try the meditation with an object with which you share a more difficult history. Again, follow the meditation with the writing exercise.

Take one of the objects you focused on (preferably one with good-natured associations) with you on your next astral trip. Hold the object near your chest link as you emit the internal aether necessary to create your projected astral body and form a comparable astral counterpart from the aether of the object you've selected. Bring this phantom along with you on your journey and notice if it changes as you move through the aether. Do its emotional properties lend it any new attributes—a different appearance or texture? Does it seem larger than usual? Is this size difference due to the great importance you've placed on the object? Has the object gained a personality of its own? Consider it all with an open mind.

Try this type of experiment with other objects and see what you discover. As you gain experience traveling with phantoms, you'll learn more about aetheric doubles in general. This knowledge will serve you well in the aether, where we are surrounded with just as many objects as we are here on earth.

REACHING OUT

You may have practiced your meditations indoors since beginning your study of mentalism. If so, this exercise, which takes place outdoors, will be a welcome change. If you are already experienced in outdoor meditation, I hope you'll appreciate the subtle differences between this exercise and your regular sessions.

Your travels in the aether have no doubt led to encounters with one or more of the beings that make their home in the astral world. In this exercise, you will learn specific ways to seek out these spiritual inhabitants.

As mentioned previously, the notions we carry with us about familiar places in the material world color our perception of those places when we visit them in the aether. While more advanced mentalists can compensate for this phenomenon and even use it to their advantage, beginning students are better off steering clear of sites too familiar lest their memories interfere with their perception of the aether there. The exercise outlined next will introduce you to a new site and allow you to make some preliminary observations about the place without getting as wrapped up in it as we do with the places we visit every day, such as our homes or workplaces.

Exercise 26: Sensing Spirits

Take an afternoon and evening for the first portion of this exercise and try to get out of town if you can. Pack some food and take a notebook or tape recorder, as well as a flashlight. Go for a drive to a place you've never been before, somewhere with lots of open space that's been that way for a long time. State and national parks are usually a good choice for the type of meditation you'll be trying. If you don't live near any such parks, choose a place in a field or in the wilderness where you are unlikely to be disturbed. Arrive a few hours before sundown.

Once you've found a suitable area, hike out away from the car and any other people who might be around. You'll need your full attention focused away from the material world and its peoples and doings, so get out there and find a nice quiet spot.

Spend the rest of the day there. Eat your food, wander around, look at things, listen for the natural sounds of the place. What do you notice? What does the air smell like here? How is this place unique? Also consider how this place makes you feel. More energetic? Less inhibited? Apprehensive? Take some notes on all these things by writing in your notebook or speaking softly into your tape recorder. As the sun goes down, how does the environment change? What sounds come with dusk? Do new animals emerge? Keep observing and writing down notes about what you discover.

Keep your senses alert as the sun sets and the first stars begin to blink above. Take note of changes in the environment but also be aware of how your mood changes with the coming of night. Places usually have different effects on our psyches at night than they do during the day. Make a careful record of as many details as you can about how you feel and any conclusions you can draw from what you see, hear, and smell. Remember that this is not a psychic exercise. Use your material world senses today—there will be time for aetheric exploration later.

After you've recorded everything you've noticed about this place, walk back to the car and head for home. Think about the place you visited. Let its presence sink into your thoughts.

In order to get a good sampling of everyday reality in the spot you've chosen, you'll need to return at least a few more times for more observation. Go back at the same time of day as soon as you can—no more than a week later—and conduct more observation. Make a note of anything different you notice in yourself or the environment. If it is autumn, you may witness leaves changing or new habits among the local animals. You might even try sketching some of the details you see.

After you've visited your new place three or four times, you will have a good idea of what to expect when you go back. Review your notes and try to make any extrapolations you can about what to expect when you return. When you are finished, do something else for the rest of the day to ground your thoughts in everyday life.

The next day, at the usual time, take your notes and drive back to your place once more. As you walk from the car to your observation point, think of this: Billions of people have lived and died on this planet, and you are merely a member of one of its most recent generations. What became of the earlier inhabitants? Well, for one thing, nearly all of them are dead, passed on from this world to another, different life in the aether. Perhaps some have been reincarnated to live again in a new form, but what about those who remain in the spirit world? These are the spirits you will try to contact today.

When you can no longer notice the drone of traffic, the chatter of people, or any other indicators of humanity, stop and stand still. Even though you're alone, you're hardly the first person to ever come to this spot. Thousands of people before you have stood right here. Now it is your turn, but unlike them, you won't be hindered by time or regular perception. You won't be alone for long. You will reach out and meet those travelers who have come before you.

Have a seat on the ground or anywhere else that feels comfortable and begin the astral vibration meditation that commences all your formal aetheric sessions. Keep your eyes open if you can and pay close attention to the scene around you as you cross the threshold between the material and astral worlds. As you know, the lower astral vibration is the home of revenants and other aetheric beings with a close affinity to the material world. Pause in your meditation once you've entered the lower astral, as it is here that you're most likely to find the spirits you came to visit.

Look around. What do you see? Do all the trees and other natural features nearby seem to be where they were before and in the same shapes and arrangements? Make a mental note of anything that seems different or unexpected given what you already know about this place.

Don't be alarmed to discover spirits right away upon your arrival in the lower astral, but also don't be surprised if they take their time in showing themselves. You're a relatively new face around here, and depending on the curiosity level or shyness of the local spirits, they will either make themselves known to you quickly or gradually. Be patient, if necessary. There is no rush. There is never any rush when it comes to the dead, the inhabitants of the eternal realm.

While it might take a while for the first spirit to appear, and while there is no guarantee that it will be hospitable to you upon your first meeting, always remember to be on your best behavior, treating the spirit with as much courtesy as you would a new acquaintance in the material world. It's worth stating here that hostility is an especially dangerous thing in the aether, as it can be turned against its wielder quite effectively by more powerful aetherics. As far as this exercise is concerned, it is less important to make a new friend than it is to determine what type of spirits you encounter in this new place.

You should be able to classify the spirit quite easily after you ask yourself certain questions about it. Does the spirit appear confused or at least dazed? If so, it's likely that it is of the lost soul variety. Is the spirit preoccupied, doing something seemingly incongruous with life in the afterworld? Then you're probably in the company of a revenant. Does the spirit seem to be at ease, ecstatic, or, alternately, in agony? Perhaps you are witness to a departed spirit going through the extremes of a heaven or hell experience. Is the spirit vaporous and somewhat sinister? On the off chance that you've just met a wraith, you are advised to end your meditation session at once.

As for interaction with nonwraiths, it is truly up to you whether you interfere with their aetheric existences. Some spirits might welcome the company; others may very well wish to be left alone. When it comes to temperament, spirits are really much closer to we humans than we realize. Just like the living, some enjoy company, while others prefer solitude. Lost souls and revenants need intervention by mentalists such as yourself if they are to move on from their trapped states. Be wary but also approach these poor souls with an open heart and open mind, as you would hope someone would do for you if you were in such a situation.

Spend as much time as you like among the spirits in this place. Keep an eye out for the spirits of animals, as well as any interesting phantoms of plants or other inanimate objects. If no

spirits make themselves known to you on your first visit, don't give up. It may take another session or two before they come to you. And as always, should anything extraordinary happen while you're exploring the spirit world, please make a record of it and send a copy to this book's author.

SPIRITISM IN EVERYDAY LIFE

You now have a good idea of how to find spirits during your journeys to the astral world. The techniques you tried can work anywhere, really, but for your initial attempt it was good to get away from the hustle and bustle of everyday life. Try it again in more familiar areas such as parks and commercial areas in your hometown or even in your own neighborhood. Just remember: If you'd rather not know the souls who still inhabit your house or those nearby, it's up to you to keep from investigating these areas.

Spirits Surround Us

Just as your first steps into the astral world changed your mind about so many things you'd taken for granted in your life, so your new knowledge of the spirit world should give you an equally new perspective on reality. We are surrounded not only by people and animals in everyday life, but also by so many *things*. More than ever, the world is filled to bursting with manufactured objects of countless origins.

Take some time to consider the objects you surround yourself with in everyday life. Where do they come from? What is their material lineage? By what means are they transformed from their original components to the form they now take in your possession?

Likewise, what sort of interactions do you undertake with the natural world, the plants and animals that live in your neighborhood? It is good to get to know them better, on a spiritual level, for just as the air and water sustain both us and these beings, an even finer substance connects us all.

Remember, too, that you can improve your understanding of the spirit world merely through more conscious interaction with the people around you. By now you realize that a person doesn't have to die before you can get to know their spirit. Cherish your friendships here on earth. Learn from them and let your experiences in the material and aetheric worlds inform one another so that you are constantly developing mentally and spiritually.

Even You

Benjamin Franklin is noted for his remark that nothing in life is certain save death and taxes. While this author is unqualified to counsel its readers on the latter, I do hope that you have found enough in this lesson to stimulate thoughts on your own mortality. We all live, and if that is so, then it is equally certain that one day we shall all die. Someday, even you will become a full member of the spirit world.

Keep this in mind as you explore this fascinating place and meet the souls that live there. Think of your voyages as an early glimpse of the afterlife and of yourself as a fortunate guest in this mysterious, powerful realm.

MENS AGITAT MOLEM

LESSON SIX.
MENTAL INFLUENCE

Visualizing the Invisible—A Complete Picture—The Shape of Thoughts—Emotions Illustratated—The Nature of Thought-Form Elementals—Clairvoyance and Aetheric Gradation—A Clairvoyant Exploration—Telekinetic Influence and Emotion—Bowls of Emotion—Further Telekinetic Experiments—The Thought-Clouds of Telepathy—Telepathic Conversation—The Unspoken Message—The Ethics of Mentalism

"If the doors of perception were cleansed everything would appear to man as it is, infinite."
—WILLIAM BLAKE, *The Marriage of Heaven and Hell*

THROUGHOUT YOUR STUDIES of aether and mentalism, you've read time and again that everything existing in the world around you—people, landscapes, everyday objects—dwells also on the aetheric plane. There, too, exist thoughts, emotions, and other seemingly abstract things like time or the cultural impact of actions and objects. These things, insubstantial even in the material world, are easily observed and manipulated by the skilled mentalist. When you are in the aether, thoughts are as visible as a hand before your face, emotions can be felt as if they were rain

or wind (or even a hailstorm), and you can share sensory awareness and mental insights with others, even those long dead or
not yet born.

In this lesson, you will learn more about the three basic psychic feats of mentalism, also known as *psychisms*. These psychisms are clairvoyance (extrasensory perception of material and
aetheric traits), telekinesis (the manipulation of aetheric and
physical material using the power of the mind), and telepathy
(the sending and sensing of thoughts). The key to each of these
deeds lies in a keen perception of the subtleties of your personal
aether and the aether around you. Through simple exercises, you
will see that although these mental abilities may seem to be the
stuff of fantasy, they are all rooted in the objects, feelings, and
thoughts we interact with every day.

VISUALIZING THE INVISIBLE

It is simple enough to comprehend that your physical body—
with its arms, legs, torso, and head—exists in parallel on the
aetheric plane. The place where you are reading this book, be it
indoors or out, is easily understood to be mirrored in the aether.
If there is a physical table here, an aetheric table exists there, too.
The same trees and stones you may see from where you are also
stand firmly in the aether.

But there is more to your body than static parts—there are
processes, too. Blood flows through your veins. Your nerves relay
messages from one part of yourself to another. Individual cells
that comprise your organs are born, live, and die. The wood in
the table ages, as do the pages of this book, becoming impercep-
tibly more brittle as time passes. The trees pass through the
stages of the year and grow, and the stones are ever so slowly
worn by weather and time. All this happens in tandem on the

aetheric plane, and perhaps it is no great feat of imagination for you to understand this.

These are examples of things and processes directly observable in the material plane. But if all of life were made of what is merely observable, how strange the world would seem! We would witness actions, but not consider the motives behind them or the consequences they might bring about. In such a place there would be no feeling of love, for example, nor any sense of belonging to a family or a community. Even a rudimentary sensation, such as hunger, wouldn't exist. We would see a table, but the word "table," a very simple thought, would not come to mind. In fact, there would be no mind to speak of! The world would seem like a simulacrum, a lifeless shadow-place. We could not recognize such a world as being "real." How then, do we convince ourselves that our observations of material things and processes show us all there is to see in the aether?

Exercise 27: A Complete Picture

You can familiarize yourself with how much goes unnoticed in everyday life. Go by yourself to a small, furnished room; an office or a bedroom in a house works well for this exercise or perhaps the very room you've used for your practice of the aetheric dozen. Close any doors or window blinds that would otherwise let in views from another part of the world. Stand in the middle of the room and slowly turn around, taking in everything you can see. Try to create a basic mental inventory—floor, walls, ceiling, desk, bookshelf, door, window, books, cup (perhaps containing coffee), pens, paper, and so on. Some of the objects may be engaged in the process of electrification: fans turning, lamps emitting light. Add this process, electrification, to your inventory. Also add any wind, light, temperature changes, and sounds created by the electrified machines.

You can see how quickly such a task becomes daunting. The mind reels when we stop and think of all the things and processes that exist in one small, furnished room, and this is not even considering the solitary person in it. Blood flow and synaptic actions must be added to the inventory, to be sure, as well as thinking, and beyond that, thinking about thinking!

As you can see, this sort of observation reveals much more to you than is perceptible in your everyday life. With practice, your ability to see aetherically will open your capacity for amazing feats of mentalism.

THE SHAPE OF THOUGHTS

In the aether, thoughts and emotions emerge from our aetheric bodies and move into the common space around us, where they can be viewed, heard, even touched and related to as if they were living things independent of their creator.

Do you subscribe to a newspaper? One of the most entertaining portions of a major newspaper is the Sunday comics section. Did you know that you can catch a glimpse into the aether each time you read these comic strips?

Although today's comics are more sedate than those of years gone by, you can still find examples of what American cartoonist Mort Walker called symbolia—the circles, lines, and other shapes drawn near characters in comic strips to indicate speed, frustration, surprise, and other conditions.

Walker codified these symbols that are now clichés of the comic-strip form. If you see a cloud of dust behind a running character, you are viewing a *briffit*. Someone working hard or enduring a stressful situation may be drawn with *plewds*, exaggerated sweat droplets bursting around their head. *Emanata* shoot forth in a similar way from the heads of surprised characters, and *squeans* seem to rise and pop above those who are drunk.

Designers incorporate similar devices into their work when trying to evoke a particular emotion or state of mind. Shapes which taper from a wide base to a narrow top elicit a sense of strength in a way similar to the pyramids of ancient Egypt. Rounded forms calm us, reminding us of clouds, perhaps, or the comforting arms of a parent.

Of course, these simple forms are, like all illustrations, gross simplifications of that which they attempt to represent. However, they give us a jumping-off point for further examination of how ideas and feelings, invisible by their very nature, can be seen.

Exercise 28: Emotions Illustrated

Carry a small, unlined notepad and a pen in your pocket for a week and try this experiment. Whenever you notice yourself experiencing an emotion or a particular state of mind, be it impatience, curiosity, fatigue, or anything else, bring out your notepad and make a few abstract doodles that seem to fit with your mood. Make a note of the emotion you've just illustrated and add any pertinent notes for later reference. You might find that some experiences bring forth multiple sensations. For example, you might stub your toe on a piece of furniture, giving rise to many feelings, including surprise, pain, and frustration.

If you keep close track of the particulars of each experience, you will get a better sense of how you tend to visualize thoughts and emotions. This will serve you well in your visits to the aetheric plane, a place where everything can be seen.

The Nature of Thought-Form Elementals

When mentalists concentrate strongly for a sustained period of time on any one subject, they run the risk of their thought-aether gaining sentience and a will of its own. A renegade thought is an aetheric being known as a thought-form elemental.

Thought-form elementals are the embodiment of our ideas and ideals. They take our emotions and intentions beyond our individual human limits and make changes in the aether that can affect earthly life. Like breeds like, and the more of one emotion or state you have in your life (love, greed, envy), the more that state will naturally occur.

Lesser incarnations of thought-form elementals are actually quite common in our lives. Whenever we feel so strongly about something that our emotion "carries us away," or each time we are "lost" in thought, we are actually in the grasp of a concentrated mass of aether that, while not quite as powerful as a thought-form elemental, is still potent enough to override our own senses (or at least our common sense).

Thoughts sensed via aetheric sight might appear differently to two mentalists standing side by side. To one mentalist, a thought might appear as a puff of smoke blowing out of its thinker's mouth or forehead. To another, this same thought might look like a geometric pattern surrounding its creator. At times of great stress or concentration, thought and thinker can seem as one, an amalgam that combines human traits of the thinker and the abstract aspects of the thought. Visions of supernatural beings as varied as deific incarnations and were-wolves are thought of by some as examples of these thinker/thought combinations.

Because of the vagaries of perception, which have to do with many things including experience, culture, and spiritual beliefs, it is impossible to set hard and fast guidelines for recognizing this or that thought. Entires branches of psychology and art are devoted to the study of symbols and their meanings. Alchemy and the mystical paths of the world's religions are also rife with explorations of practical symbolism. If you are already studying such a tradition, it will no doubt shape the way you perceive aether. If you aren't, and if you are having trouble making sense of abstract perceptions in the aether, it may behoove you to explore one or more of these systems.

CLAIRVOYANCE AND
AETHERIC GRADATION

So far in your studies of mentalism you have learned of clairvoy-ance as a means of transferring your earthly senses—sight, hear-ing, and so forth—beyond the confines of your physical body. In itself, this is much akin to astral projection. In this essay, you will learn of a different sort of clairvoyance—one that can give you insight into the nature, history, and impact of the objects we see every day.

In order to understand how this clairvoyance works, you'll need a better understanding of the multifaceted nature of aether. There are many aetheric aspects to even the simplest of ordinary objects. If we look at a pen, for example, we can see that it is made of material substance such as wood, metal, or plastic. It has a cap, perhaps, of the same substance. The pen also contains ink.

It is simple enough to understand that all this material is mirrored in the aether. On the aetheric plane a pen made of metal, for example, is made of an equal "mass" of the intangible aether. There is aether for the pen's main body, aether for the cap, aether for the tube containing the ink, and aether for the ink itself.

That said, there is more to see in this pen than the aether of its physical components. Ore was mined from the earth to create the metal from which the pen is fashioned. The ink, too, came from a natural source. These sources can be discovered through clairvoyant sight. Many hands went into the manufacture of the pen. Aside from those who gathered the raw materials, there was at least one maker, a person who put the pen together. For every individual involved in the pen's making, there is a bit of his or her personal aether in the pen. If you are the first owner of the pen, then you know what has been written with it. Perhaps it doesn't require any meditation at all to remember the shopping lists, the phone messages, and the letters you've written using this device. If the pen isn't brand new, however, you can use clairvoyance to learn what writings have come from the pen before it came into your possession.

Such feats of mentalism are possible because of the range of frequencies contained in the aether. In past exercises, you've been directed to modulate the frequency of your personal aether from its normal material-world state to that of the astral and elemental realms. It is also possible to attain the ultimate frequency, that of the elysian. Each of these gradations in your personal aether brings about a different state of mind in you, a different state of being.

It may surprise you that pedestrian objects have the same sorts of variance in their own aether. Here is a comparative listing of the aspects of various gradations of aether, as relates to a simple metal pen.

Material Aether: The physical mass and makeup of the pen is reflected in the aether most readily visible by mentalists when they first tune their consciousness to the aetheric plane. Anything having to do with size, shape, color, weight, or other physical dimensions or measurements is the business of the realm of the material aether.

Elemental Aether: When we reduce the frequency of our awareness below the normal confines of the material-world range of the aether, we reach a consciousness of the elemental world. This is the realm of fire, air, water, and earth or a combination of two or more of these elements, such as steam, metal, magma, or dust. Any aether we observe here reflects the earthly origins of the object before us, telling us what form its parts were in before the object's manufacture. In the case of the pen, this would include the rocky ore from which the pen's metal was smelted, any of the natural or chemical beginnings of various details on the pen (a different metal for the clip on the cap, perhaps, or plastic for the interior tube, or the paint used to mark the manufacturer's seal), and the source of the pen's ink.

Astral Aether: When we raise our consciousness to the aetheric frequencies higher than the material realm, we find ourselves in the astral world. This is the place where thoughts and emotions reign, where we can see with our mind's eye those things that we most often think of as intangible. Viewing the pen while in an astral state of mind will reveal the intellectual and emotional conditions of its manufacture, as well as whatever writings have come from the pen. The astral world is seemingly boundless, and there is much contained in the astral aether of everyday objects. Therefore, it may take quite a few aetheric sessions to discover all there is to know about the astral aspects of your seemingly simple pen.

Elysian Aether: The highest of all aetheric frequencies lies in the elysian world, also known as Elysium. This is the realm of the shared consciousness of the earth and the planets and stars beyond it, and it is also the most difficult place to reach in your meditations. Here, we can stand among the heroes and gods of all cultures, as well as the group-soul of current and past civilizations. What does this have to do with the prosaic pen before you? Nothing, perhaps, but it depends on the pen's historical and cultural importance. With an elysian attentiveness, you can become aware of the influence this pen has on the world as a whole. Perhaps it was used to write an important piece of legislation or even a love letter between two people who went on to change the course of history, such as Napoleon and Joséphine.

Exercise 29: A Clairvoyant Exploration
Practice such clairvoyant observation of an everyday item during your next meditation. Sit with the object before you, preferably resting on a table or other flat surface, so you can see it without holding it. Concentrate on your breath and shift your awareness to the aetheric plane. You are there, and the object is there with you. If you are recording your session either through audio or

written notes—perhaps even with the help of a secretary—describe the object you see as it exists in the material aether. What are its clearly observable dimensions and characteristics?

Take as long as you like with the object, modulating your aetheric attention among the various realms. Record your observations in each of these states. With practice, your clairvoyant examinations of even the simplest items will likely yield surprising discoveries!

TELEKINETIC INFLUENCE AND EMOTION

Just after you began your practice of the aetheric dozen, you used your new knowledge of the aetheric links—points of connection between a person's physical and sublime bodies—to conduct a very simple, yet nonetheless astounding, telekinetic experiment. If the exercise was successful, you were able to move a coin a fraction of an inch using nothing but the power of your mind.

Whether or not this exercise worked for you, your curiosity about telekinesis is no doubt piqued. We will now explore further mechanics and applications of this most extraordinary mental practice.

When we talk of telekinesis, we are speaking of feats of mind over matter. In a very basic way, this is something we do every day. Every time we go for a walk, answer a ringing telephone, tie our shoes, or do any number of seemingly mundane tasks, we are applying our mental forces to move our bodies and manipulate the objects around us. Some days this is easy, and other days it is a chore to do the simplest thing.

As it is in the everyday, material world, so it is in the aether. The reasons most aspiring mentalists fail in their telekinetic attempts are akin to why they also have trouble getting out of bed in the morning. They are tired, perhaps, or they are bored. They see no compelling reason to get up and start the day. They feel unchallenged by the life they have arranged for themselves. These same people will never find themselves to be effective telekinetics until they discover their own reason for being in the material world. Without this, what business do they have nosing around in the aether? Anyone who wishes to show off telekinetic ability by levitating people or causing household objects to fly to his or her hand is likely lacking in the willpower to lift these things physically. How, then, do they expect success as a mentalist? It baffles.

The wise aspirant realizes that such feats are less desirable than the more subtle effects telekinetic ability can have on our inner life, particularly as regards our emotions. The motivation needed for any particular action in the material world arises out of our desires and emotions, and it is this same part of ourselves that makes telekinesis possible.

The exercises that follow deal with observation of your emotions. It is best to practice these exercises as the emotions arise naturally, not creating false circumstances to bring the emotion to the forefront of your consciousness. It is also important to remember that the moments you feel the strongest emotion often coincide with instances of physical strain or danger. Your safety is of the utmost importance, so please do not attempt this or any other mentalism work if you are in a situation where the more prudent act would be to remove yourself from harm's way. That said, let's move on.

Have you ever felt an emotion so strongly that it seemed to have a life of its own or at least a form that you could sense within your body? In moments of danger or surprise we sometimes seize up, stunned by the sudden turn of events. When we fall in love, our hearts feel as though they will burst. A similar feeling comes over us during times of tremendous grief.

It is easy to dismiss these sensations as instinctual reactions contained solely within your physical body, but the truth is that when you feel such things you are actually subconsciously shaping your personal aether into forms that can be mentally manipulated by yourself and others.

Exercise 30: Bowls of Emotion

If you have been practicing the exercise in which you jot down notes and doodles on your everyday thoughts and sudden surges of emotion, then it is a simple matter to expand it into a practical telekinetic feat. Review the doodles and sketches you have made out of your experiences with different emotions. Have you found that one or more emotions elicit consistent pictures? Do you feel the same sort of physical sensation each time the emotion occurs? If so, this emotion is ripe for aetheric study.

The next time you feel overwhelmed by this particular feeling, try this exercise. Stand up straight, your feet about shoulder distance apart and your arms at your sides, just as you do at the beginning of each of your sessions with the aetheric dozen. Bring your consciousness to the aetheric plane. Feel the earth beneath your feet and ground yourself in this place, no matter how jumbled or lost you may feel.

Now open your eyes (you may open just your aetheric eyes if you wish, keeping your physical eyes closed) and look at the scene before you and around you. What do you see? The color and form of the emotion manifesting itself should be familiar to you, given your preparatory sketchbook work. Perhaps your feelings are exhibiting themselves in a jumble of chaotic shapes and colors swarming around your head, maybe even surrounding your entire body. Or it could be that your emotion is blinding you to everything but a particular color, such as red or black. Are there sounds associated with this state, noises that you know aren't coming from outside sources? Do the sounds create their own shapes in the aether? Pause until you're able to observe the emotion clearly and calmly.

Keeping your elbows where they are, lift your forearms up with your palms facing out. It is a gesture of surrender, but you may be surprised at how this particular form of giving in will help you. Visualize your forehead and hand aetheric links, the links used most often in works of telekinesis.

In order to perform this exercise, you need to gather all of the turbulent emotional aether into the space in front of you, where you can see it. Extend your arms out from your sides, your palms still facing forward. Now pivot at the waist to the left and reach a little more to this direction. Gather up some of the aether that is to your sides and back with this motion and, pivoting back to your original position, bring it before you. Repeat this movement to the right. Remember to use broad, slow, and open movements. What you are doing could be likened to raking leaves, an activity unrewarded by sharp, fast actions.

It may take a while to bring all the aether before you and keep it there, and the very act of working with the aether in this way can elicit an emotional response of its own. Carry on with the exercise to the best of your ability until you have collected it all.

Once this is done, bring your arms back to your sides and face your palms out as before. Now, from the aetheric link in your right hand, send a line of blue flame out in an arc to your right. This line should go out far enough to encompass the entire mass of aether before curving back to meet the aetheric link in your left hand. It should seem that the aether is now captured in an arcing band made of your own creation.

Send out another such line from your forehead link up and across the top of the mass of aether. Once it has reached the far side, loop it beneath the mass and back toward your forehead.

When you have done this, you will see that you have formed two perpendicular bands around the aether. The emotion that once controlled you is now subdued and can be shaped by you, instead of the other way around.

Using your visualization skills, construct latticework between the bands, such that a cage is built around the aether. When this is done, slowly begin shrinking the cage and the aether held prisoner within it. You are concentrating the aether. If you keep this up, you will eventually have a sphere of aether about the size of a softball floating before you. Bring it close to you and, when it is within a foot of your chest, reach out, take the sphere into your hands, and dissolve the cage. The renegade aether is now under your command and will not hurt you.

Like all aether, this sphere is malleable like clay. Using your aetheric hands, sculpt the sphere into a small bowl. Work with the shape until it is very firm in your hands, until you know that this aether is no longer hatred or jealousy or whatever emotion it has been but is a tool for you to use. Like attracts like in the aether, and this bowl can be brought out to collect similar emotional aether the next time you feel the same sort of negative feelings rising up in you. Aether collected in this way can be easily dissipated, such that it will not bother you. It can also be transformed, through visualization, into a more beneficial emotion. An aspirant's collection of aether based on a particular emotion—love is a common example—will bring more of the same emotion to that mentalist.

When you are ready to be finished with the bowl, loosen your grip and move your hands slightly farther apart. Now, slowly draw the aether of the bowl into your hand links, reincorporating it with your personal aether.

It will be to your advantage to create many aetheric bowls to catch and hold the various emotions you experience. To make a

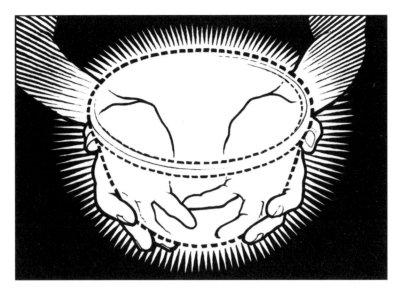

rather mundane comparison, these bowls can be used aetherically in the same way you use containers to store the uneaten portions of a meal. After all, we're all just as susceptible to being washed away by good feelings as we are in loading up on too much rich food, which can give us indigestion. And besides, you never know when you'll need to bring out one of these bowls and help yourself to a leftover serving of love, cheerfulness, or satisfaction.

Exercise 31: Further Telekinetic Experiments

As you progress in your understanding of the aether, return to your initial telekinetic experiment, in which you moved the coin, however slightly. Practice it until it takes less and less effort to move the coin. If you like, you may try to lift the coin or move it horizontally through space, but there is really no need for this—these things are easy enough to do by hand. But what more can you do with a small object like the coin? Based on your understanding of the grades of aether from this lesson's essay on clairvoyance, you know that this simple lump of metal contains more than meets the eye. Everything on the aetheric plane contains various aspects (form, history, cultural significance, and so on) within its multilayered aether. Tuning in to the physical aether of an object allows you to telekinetically affect its physical aspects such as location, color, shape, density, and arrangement of parts. What possibilities lie in the mental manipulation of that same object's elemental aether or its astral or even its elysian aether? Experiment with these aspects for yourself and see what happens.

THE THOUGHT-CLOUDS OF TELEPATHY

So far in your studies of mentalism we have only touched on the topic of telepathy, the aetheric method of communication. Here we will go into how a person's thoughts appear in the aether and how they can be sent and received with ease.

When we talk to one another face-to-face in everyday life, we use the medium of speech. In such a conversation, ideas are transmitted through the use of words spoken by one person and heard by another. Additionally, many unspoken messages are transferred between people through body language, context, and tone of voice. On the aetheric plane, we have no need for such material-world conventions as speech and gesture, but there are other means by which we can converse. There, a thought emanates not audibly from our mouths but visibly from our personal aether—the aether that makes up what we call our self. Usually this emanation occurs around the head portion of the personal aether, but thoughts can also be seen coming from other areas such as the hands, the stomach, or the sex organs, depending on the nature of the idea. Once you are able to see thoughts this way, you may be amazed at how clear conversation becomes!

Our thoughts drift, cloudlike, from ourselves into the space around us. Weak or frivolous thoughts, such as internal commentary about things or people seen on the street, evaporate almost immediately, dissipating like mist and leaving us with scant memory of ever having thought them. Remember, though, that nothing ever vanishes completely on the aetheric plane. Just like matter in the physical world, in this parallel place there is only so much aether, and while a portion of the stuff may change shape, color, size, and even function, traces of its previous embodiments always remain. Strong thoughts, such as ruminations on significant occurrences in our lives, hover around our bodies like clouds, sometimes wrapping themselves around us more in the manner of a cloak. Or they imprint themselves on our aetheric bodies in such a way that we cannot be seen without our thoughts there, plain as day and perhaps less than flattering—"written across our face," as it were. We can be free of these thoughts and their effects only through intense personal work. The strongest of thoughts may never detach completely from our personal aether and can preoccupy our thoughts to the point of distracting us from everyday existence. Storms of frivolous thought can do this, too. When we are "lost in the clouds" in this way while walking, we may trip over a stone in the road. If driving a car, we may not notice that the stoplight has turned to red.

Our thoughts are at their strongest the moment we think them. Once we become aware of a thought, it has already begun the process of detaching itself from our personal aether and moving into the surrounding space. We speed this departure markedly when we blurt out our every thought to those around us, but the truth is that any communication—every bit of speech or gesture, every piece of artwork—has a dissociating effect on our thought and dilutes its potency as something purely our own. Although to be fair, in the aether there is very little that we can truly call our own, either.

As an aspiring mentalist, you will do well to notice your thoughts at the moment of their inception, in the hopes of making clearer mental imagery to send through the aether. Practice holding your thoughts at the forefront of your mind without expressing them in speech or any form of gesture. As you continue this practice, pause to reflect on each thought you are holding. What are the qualities of the thought? Use your knowledge of the aether to apply visual aspects such as shape and color to the thought. Once you are able to do this as second nature, you will be ready to try the following experiments.

Exercise 32: Telepathic Conversation

Arrange to meet with a friend, preferably one who is interested in mentalism and is at the same point that you are in your aetheric studies. Have a simple conversation together. Talk about everyday activities such as grocery shopping or washing the dishes. This conversation should have no more than four or five statements from each person. With each statement you make out loud, form a mental image out of the corresponding thought and send it forth, away from your personal aether toward your friend. They should do the same. Keep track of your impressions of your friend's statements as they make them and note any aetheric observations you have about the images they are sending you. This is not a simple exercise, as it requires not just powerful thinking, as well as thinking about thinking, but also thinking about another person's thoughts on thinking. If you try this experiment a number of times with your friend and again a few times with another friend, you will understand not only how to better notice thoughts in the aether, but you will also begin to see how one person's thoughts look and feel different from another's.

Exercise 33: The Unspoken Message

Is there someone in your life whom you talk with every day—someone you live with or work with, perhaps? Maybe a bus driver or someone who works at a coffee shop you visit on a daily basis? You can test your ability to send telepathic messages with this person. It is important not to let them know you are doing anything of the sort, however, as this will influence the experiment.

The next time you speak with this person, bring a simple message to the forefront of your thoughts, something brief and clear and appropriate to the setting in which you know them. For a store clerk or a bus driver you might think, "Ask me about my handbag." For someone you live or work with you could think, "Buy us some flowers." You must think this same thought exactly several times, so keep it as simple as possible. After you have finished your regular conversation with that person and have said goodbye, think the thought again while visualizing the person's face. Send this same thought into the aether several times while you two are apart, each time seeing the person's face in your mind. Say it a few times just before you see them again the next day, and once more when you're speaking with them.

Don't bring up the object of your thought in your spoken conversation with them. If they do ask you about your handbag or bring in flowers, you'll know that your message may have been received. If you feel comfortable doing so, you can tell them about your experiment. Try another and see what happens!

THE ETHICS OF MENTALISM

Some people, when reading about the practice of mentalism and its capacity to grant the aspirant untold power, believe that the coursework outlined in this book is providing instruction in some form of black magic. That is to say, they believe that once an aspiring mentalist gains control of his personal aether and the aether around himself, he will become selfish and destructive, eager to hold this newfound influence over the wills of other people. If I believed this claim to be unreasonable, then I would not feel moved to write this word of caution.

The majority of aspirants to mentalism go on to lead their aetheric lives in an ethical way. But, it is true, some who have tapped into the aether have turned its power to their own advantage over others. They eavesdrop on the thoughts of friends and strangers, make unbidden astral visits, and use mentalism to brainwash or otherwise dominate others. These uses of the aether are unethical and, as these twisted mentalists will discover, destructive not only to their victims but also to themselves.

Given all you've been through in your aetheric studies, you now realize that we are not the isolated individuals, as so many people in the material world would wish us to believe. We are connected by the substance of life itself—the aether. Just as the oceans support life on earth, the aether connects and nourishes us all. And like the ocean, too, the aether can drown countless people without a second thought.

Once we realize that we have a human soul that lives within us and represents us on the aetheric plane, and that this soul transcends not only material existence but also all material concerns—including mortality—we should as a matter of course lead lives of goodness and responsibility toward ourselves and others. Our souls are all connected in the aether. Any gain that comes to an individual at the expense of others is an offense against the whole and will be revisited upon its instigator in the same way disease comes to us when we mistreat our material forms. Keep this connectedness in mind as you practice your mentalism. The techniques and abilities you are developing bring you closer to everything in creation, a place we all share.

In your day-to-day dealings with those around you, you may have already discovered that the smallest courtesy goes a long way in improving people's disposition toward you. People tend not to be bad-hearted, as such, but every one of us has a capacity to withdraw into ourselves and focus on our wishes and needs over those of others. A simple hello to our neighbor, a smile to someone we pass on the street, or a small, unasked-for favor for someone we know—each of these acts is a very powerful way of breaking through not only the needless defensive screens people put up around themselves, but through our own shells as well.

As you begin to open yourself in this way, you will realize how susceptible each of us is to the influences of our surroundings, the other people in our lives, and our own personal thoughts and emotions. At the same time, you will see more clearly the ties between yourself, other people, and the world, and you will grow in your understanding of the aether in a healthy, nondestructive way.

INDEX OF EXERCISES BY
NUMBER AND TITLE

INDEX OF EXERCISES
BY TOPIC

ACKNOWLEDGMENTS

DEEPEST GRATITUDE goes to my parents, Craig and Lana Marsh, and my brother, Kirk Marsh, for teaching me kindness, encouraging my curiosity, and always believing in me. Also to Jeff Hoke for his generous companionship throughout the creation of this book. Beyond Jeff's tremendous work as my illustrator and editor, his friendship, insight, and easygoing humor about the most arcane (and mundane!) subjects have been constant sources of inspiration and rejuvenation.

Thank you to Anandamayi Arnold for her love and encouragement. To Laramie Crocker, Wendi Olson, and the Cammell-Brown family for daily support and friendship. To Brenda Knight and all the other good people at Weiser for their faith and hard work. To Heather Schlegel for her support of my early work on this project. To all the friends who served as models for the illustrations or who gave comments on essays. And last but certainly not least, to my regular aetheric correspondents S. C., R. D., and A. R., and to all the patient aspirants who subscribe to *The Camelopard*. There is yet more on its way to all of you!

ABOUT THE AUTHOR

CLINT MARSH is a writer and publisher of practical esoterica. Aside from *The Camelopard*—the pamphlet series that inspired this book—Marsh's publications include *Goblinproofing One's Chicken Coop, On Gnoming (A Pocket Guide to the Successful Hunting and Cooking of Gnomes),* and *Wandering Wizards Welcome (By Appointment).* He has served as the consulting editor for Jeff Hoke's *Guide to Lost Wonder* series and as the American publisher for *Phooka, The Journal of the Overland Mallet Club.* He lives in Berkeley, California, and distributes his works through Wonderella Printed.

TO OUR READERS